# SAVORY
# SOUPS & STEWS

*Italian Pepperoni Minestrone, page 82*

# SAVORY
# SOUPS & STEWS

RODALE

Printed in the United States of America
Rodale Inc. makes every effort to use acid-free ∞, recycled paper ♲.

*Cover photograph:* markthomasstudio.com
*Cover recipe:* 30-Minute Chili,
              Courtesy of McIlhenny Company, page 20
*Food stylist:* Diane Vezza
*Illustrations:* Judy Newhouse

Produced by:
BETH ALLEN ASSOCIATES, INC.

*President/Owner:* Beth Allen
*Designer:* Monica Elias
*Art Production Director:* Laura Smyth (smythtype)
*Culinary Consultant/Food Editor:* Deborah Mintcheff
*Food Writer:* Jean Galton
*Copy Editor:* Brenda Goldberg
*Public Relations Consultants:* Stephanie Avidon, Melissa Moritz
*Nutritionist:* Michele C. Fisher, Ph.D., R.D.

**Library of Congress Cataloging-in-Publication Data**

Savory soups & stews.
       p.   cm.
    Includes index.
    ISBN 1–57954–951–9   hardcover, tqc
    ISBN 1–59486–061–0   hardcover, qtf
    1. Soups.  2. Stews.  I. Rodale Press.
 TX757 .S3 2004
    641.8′13—dc22                    2003024421

 2 4 6 8 10 9 7 5 3   hardcover, tqc
 2 4 6 8 10 9 7 5 3 1 hardcover, qtf

WE **INSPIRE** AND **ENABLE** PEOPLE TO IMPROVE
THEIR LIVES AND THE WORLD AROUND THEM

FOR MORE OF OUR PRODUCTS

WWW.RODALESTORE.COM
(800) 848-4735

# CONTENTS

# INTRODUCTION

## *When's a good time for homemade soups?*

Anytime! Homemade soups always seem to be a great idea. Remember the good feeling of a steaming bowl of chicken noodle soup when you were a kid? With the freshly made noodles, the rich broth, and those juicy bites of chicken? And those creamy chowders at the seashore and that French soup, dripping with cheese, in the little bistro? They're still around—and they're still brimming over with all of their homemade goodness. Now you can fix them faster and easier than ever before. All it takes is a few simple ingredients and this book, filled with 100 ways to make soups and stews speedier and simpler. Bring them back into your soup pot, even for supper tonight.

Thumb through this collection of *Savory Soups & Stews*. You're likely to find an instant answer to what's for tonight's supper by checking out the super-fast recipes. Just look for the SuperQuick label. Each soup or stew goes from "shopping bag to table" in 30 minutes or less! Choose the Mac 'n' Double-Cheese Soup (page 93), and you'll be in and out of the kitchen even faster, in just 20 minutes flat. Or simmer up an old-fashioned Turkey Vegetable Soup with bow-tie pasta (page 36)…a kettle of Chicken & Red Pepper Corn Chowder (page 54)…a Hearty Tortellini Pot from the Italian countryside (page 42).

Some other night, invite over a few friends and simmer up supper all in one pot. Discover hearty Beefy Meal-in-a-Pot (page 102)…a fast-and-easy pot of Shrimp Creole (page 107)…and the Best-Ever Chicken Noodle (page 120), perfect for simmering "on its own," low and slow some weekend. We haven't forgotten that handy crockpot. Toss in the fixings for our Spicy Ham-Chili Crockpot (page 106) in the morning, turn on the pot, and walk back to supper at night.

Like our other quick-cooking books, you'll quickly see that *Savory Soups & Stews* is much more than just another recipe book. It's filled with fresh ideas for filling up the soup pot as well as practical tried-and-true advice you'll turn to often. Start off by thumbing through the first chapter, "Tastier Soups & Stews." You'll find six exciting techniques for soups and stews which are brimming over with goodness and flavor. One shows you how to simmer up a homemade stock in an hour (that's 75 percent less time then your grandmother took). Another gives four ways to pile the flavor into the kettle, such as marinating meat before adding it to the pot. And still another offers three ways to layer in and build up the flavors of your favorite soup and stew recipe even more.

But that's just the beginning. We've teamed up with test kitchens of famous food manufacturers and other cooking pros from coast to coast—with one goal in mind: to bring you 100 fabulous, fast, flavor-packed recipes for soups and stews, even if you're just learning to cook. Most are from the "school" of fix-and-forget it": toss the ingredients into the pot and walk away as it simmers. Some recipes come with "On the Menu" ideas to help you plan what's for dinner, whatever the occasion, weekday or weekend, however little time you have. And still others come with "Cook to Cook" tips, from cooks just like you, on such topics as how to change a favorite soup recipe into a hearty dinner stew.

Throughout this book, you'll find "Cooking Basics" lessons. Check out the one on page 78 for rescuing soups and stews that are too salty, too thin, too cloudy, or just plain too watery and not tasting great. Look for TimeSaver tips to learn how to shortcut the steps (and the preparation time!) in the soup pot, without sacrificing the flavor. Plus you'll find speedy ways to jump-start the soup or stew pot, such as pre cooking meat and veggies by "Microwaving in Minutes" (which cuts simmering time in the pot later). And take a peek at page 11 to find out how to turn a quart of stock into seven fast bowls of soup.

We've tucked in a wealth of answers to common food questions, like how to save cents in the stew pot (page 75). Check out the "Food Facts" box (page 62) to find out how to add even more protein to the chowder pot. And turn to page 108 to see how Hoppin' John got its name and why it's considered a good-luck charm throughout the South.

Have fun simmering up many of the scrumptious recipes we've tucked into *Savory Soups & Stews*—and all of the great tips and food facts sifted among the pages. But that's not all! You can look forward to even more fabulous and fast cooking ideas in the other books in our collection. Each of the cook books has been created to feature a specific type of food and provide just what you want today—quick, speedy, simple, great-tasting recipes. Plus beautiful photographs, cooking techniques that work, handy preparation tips, and interesting food facts. In addition, each book in our quick-cooking collection is guaranteed to become a "reliable kitchen helper." We've designed each to be not only interesting to thumb through but also so jam-packed that you'll find yourself relying on each one time after time.

Here's to rediscovering how those homemade pots of *Savory Soups & Stews* are *faster, easier, and more foolproof than ever!*

*Brunswick Stew, page 124*

# Tastier Soups & Stews

Boil down the time needed to make those great-tasting soups and stews that Grandma used to cook by about 75 percent—while still simmering in that great homemade flavor. Start by following our six favorite quick-cooking techniques with soups and stews—with much less fuss, much more know-how, and a lot of attention to every ingredient, every seasoning, and every technique. They're all right here—straight from the cooking pros and cooks just like you. These cooks also have a lot less time today but still crave those homemade creations from yesteryear's soup kettles. So read on, and discover ways to simmer up those tasty soup and stew pots of grandmother's day—many, in a quarter of the time.

## LADLE UP THE PERFECT HOMEMADE STOCK IN LESS THAN AN HOUR!

Now you can simmer up a flavor-filled, made-from-scratch stock in 1 hour, instead of the usual four—thanks to our quick-cooking techniques. Canned broth is, of course, even quicker, and that's just fine when you're in a rush. But there's nothing quite like the flavor of a stock, soup, or stew you've made yourself! Ask any cook: a good stock on-hand gives a speedy jump-start to many soup and stew recipes.

**START WITH COLD TAP WATER** (not hot), then bring it up to a fast boil in the microwave or over high heat. Boiling water speeds up the cooking of the soup pot faster than you think. And your soup will be better tasting for it! Hot tap water contains impurities from the hot water heater that can cloud stock and give it off flavors. There's one exception: if you're lucky enough to have an instant boiling water tap, by all means, use it.

**THE BIG-LITTLE MEAT CUT UP!** Chicken, turkey, beef (in fact, any meat) releases its flavor faster as it cooks, if you cut it into small pieces before adding it to the soup pot. Ask your butcher to chop up the bird or the roast into 2-inch pieces (bones and all!). Or do it yourself with a meat cleaver.

**THE RIPER, THE BETTER!** Throw the ripest, softest veggies you can find into the soup pot. They are sweeter, and the pectins holding their cells together have already changed to softer, more soluble pectins. As vegetables cook, these pectins dissolve quickly, contributing more flavor to the pot than their less ripe "cousins." Choose the softest onions, the ripest red peppers, and some potatoes without any "green."

**OUT OF THE FREEZER INTO THE POT...** Go ahead, use frozen chicken pieces in the stock pot. Simply drop them in frozen. Don't thaw, as they'll add a fresher flavor to the pot. Just extend the simmering time about 10 minutes.

*Spicy Senegalese Soup, page 77*

*Warming Asian Soup, page 87*

*Tuscan Rice & Bean Soup, page 80*

**FAST CHICKEN STOCK—READY, SAUTÉ, SIMMER!** Sauté 3 to 4 pounds of cut-up, 2-inch chicken (or turkey) pieces on the bone (legs, thighs, or a whole bird) with a large chopped onion in a heavy soup pot. Cook about 5 minutes, or until the bird loses its pink color. Cover the pot, reduce the heat to low, and simmer for 20 minutes. Now, pour in 8 cups of boiling water and add some sprigs of fresh thyme and a dried bay leaf. Then simmer the stock some more, uncovered this time, about 30 minutes more, or until it tastes delicious. Strain. (Makes about 1 quart.)

## Cooking Basics

### THE MANY FAST "BOWLS" FROM A QUART OF STOCK

Start with our Fast Chicken Stock (recipe above this box) and create a wide wonderful world of homemade soups! They're ready to ladle up in 30 minutes or less.

**ITALIAN EGG DROP** Bring 4 cups Fast Chicken Stock to a boil. Mix 2 eggs with ¼ cup grated Parmesan cheese. Drizzle the eggs into the broth while stirring gently. Cook until the eggs are set, about 2 minutes. Season with salt, pepper, and chopped parsley.

**CHINESE CHICKEN NOODLE** Bring 4 cups Fast Chicken Stock to a boil with ½ cup sliced scallions and 2 large minced cloves of garlic. Simmer for 15 minutes. Stir in 1 tablespoon soy sauce and 3 ounces fresh noodles. Cook 2 minutes. Garnish with sliced scallions.

**WONTON SOUP** Bring 4 cups Fast Chicken Stock to a boil with 4 thin slices peeled fresh ginger and 2 large minced garlic cloves. Simmer for 15 minutes, then stir in 1 tablespoon soy sauce. Add 8 to 10 frozen dumplings and simmer 5 minutes more, or until the dumplings are tender. (If you can find freshly made dumplings, use them—but simmer only about 3 minutes.) Stir in 2 tablespoons slivered ham and sprinkle with some sliced scallions.

**ZUCCHINI, ORZO & PESTO** Bring 6 cups Fast Chicken Stock to a boil. Add 2 tablespoons orzo and cook for 7 minutes, or until almost done. Stir in 1 small thinly sliced zucchini and cook 2 minutes longer. Season with salt and pepper. Serve with a dollop of pesto (store-bought or your own).

**CREAM OF POTATO** Bring 4 cups Fast Chicken Stock to a boil. Whisk in 2 cups mashed potatoes (leftovers are just fine) and 2 tablespoons heavy cream. Simmer for 10 minutes, season with salt and white pepper, and top with a generous sprinkling of snipped chives.

**OLD-FASHIONED TOMATO BISQUE** Bring 2 cups Fast Chicken Stock to a boil. Purée one 14½-ounce can (undrained) chopped or fire-roasted tomatoes and stir in with 2 tablespoons heavy cream. Simmer for 5 minutes and season with salt and pepper. Top with toasted croutons, grated cheese, or chopped parsley.

**ROASTED RED PEPPER SOUP** Bring 2 cups Fast Chicken Stock to a boil. Puree one 7-ounce jar drained roasted peppers and stir in. Season with fresh lemon juice, salt and pepper. Top with a dollop of sour cream. Sprinkle with some snipped chives.

## PILE ON THE FLAVOR

Take a tip from the pros—and pile on the flavor as you cook soups and stews. The secret is to layer on the falvoring and seasonings, a little at a time, to build up the flavors as the pot simmers. This gives your soup or stew a much more complex, full-bodied flavor. And it all begins with your salt shaker!

**SEASON IT FIRST**—A few hours, preferably a day before, salt and spice meat and poultry before putting it into the stew pot. Rule of thumb: Use ½ teaspoon coarse salt per pound of meat and toss it to coat all sides, then cover and refrigerate. Several good-tasting things happen: the meat becomes beautifully seasoned throughout as well as more tender and moist. Osmosis draws the salt into the cell walls of the meat, pulling more moisture into the cells at the same time. Salt goes to work on the tough muscle fibers too, weakening them and tenderizing the meat. Right before cooking, add another level of seasoning by sprinkling on a little more salt and finely ground pepper too, if you like.

**MARINATE FOR MORE FLAVOR** Before getting out the stew pot, rub poultry or meat with a marinade. Refrigerate for a few hours, but not more than 4 hours, as chicken can lose its texture and turn soft in a strong marinade. For chicken, try a simple light oil and vinegar dressing…for beef, a teriyaki, steak, or barbecue sauce. This trick not only flavors up the meat, but beefs up the flavor of the entire pot, too.

**SALT & TASTE AS YOU COOK** Before each ingredient goes into the pot, quickly season and spice it. When sautéing onions, sprinkle with a little salt (plus a little sugar, too) to bring out more of their flavor. As other vegetables go into the pot, such as carrots, sprinkle them with a little salt and sugar, too. This gradual seasoning of the pot creates a more complex (and much more delicious) broth, soup, and stew. Plus, since a small amount is used at each addition, you'll end up using less salt in the finished dish!

*Pork & Pepper Stew, page 111*

*Texas Beef Stew, page 101*

*Tuna-Corn Chowdah, page 62*

*Zesty Italian Soup, page 112*

**IT'S ALL IN THE RUB!** Dry rubs are another great way to quickly add a layer of flavor to your soup pot. Make your own rub or buy one, such as the the Cajun spice mix and French herb blends in themarket. To hasten the flavoring, use more than usual: 2 tablespoons of dry rub for each 4 pounds of meat. Let the rub set for 15 minutes, instead of the usual 24 hours.

## LAYERING UP!

The more complex and "built up" the flavor of a soup or stew, the more interesting and homemade tasting it'll be. Here, three quick steps to an exciting flavor-burst in your faster-made soup pot:

• **Pick one or two ingredients, such as onions and peppers.** Sauté half of them until they turn a rich dark brown, adding browned bits and thickening.

• **Add the rest of those two ingredients toward the end** of cooking, giving crispness, color, and a little bit of crunch to the finished dish.

• **Add stock or broth a little at a time**—not all at once. This keeps the stew still cooking and browning on the bottom of the pot, instead of "poaching" in lots of liquid and turning the meat that unappetizing grayish-brown.

## ALWAYS SIMMER—NEVER BOIL THE POT

Insure your soup pot contains only succulent, moist, and tender meat—not greasy, cloudy or tough. Watch the cooking temperature! Moist meat has simmered slowly and gently, at a temperature that never rises above 185°F. Stringy tougher meat has boiled in the pot (at 212°F or higher), causing the moisture in the meat to evaporate, and the collagen proteins to melt away. These proteins are the "glue" that keeps the meat succulent and moist. It's fine to jump-start the pot by boiling water or stock at first. But then, reduce the heat to medium-low to keep the soup cooking at the right temperature. Always simmer, don't boil, from then on to prevent fat from emulsifying (combining) with the liquid soup—ensuring the stock stays clear.

## BROWN IT!

To quickly add a deeper, richer flavor in everything from chicken stock to beef stew, brown those vegetables and bones and brown them well. The sugars in vegetables caramelize on the surface, contributing color and wonderful flavor. In meats and poultry, both sugars and proteins caramelize, adding a lovely taste and a wonderful rich brown coating on the bottom of the pot. When liquid is added, the brown particles rise off the bottom of the pan and become the flavor-base of the soup or stew. The browner the coating you create (without burning), the deeper tasting your soup with be.

**A SPOONFUL OF SUGAR** When sautéing or browning onions for a soup or stew, sprinkle them with a tiny bit of sugar. It enhances the caramelization process (already in progress), deepening and enriching the flavor at the same time.

## WHIRL AWAY!

Gone are the days of having to transfer hot steaming soups to the food processor to purée—or trying to add a thickener to a bubbling stew, ending up with a lumpy mess. Reach for a hand-held immersion blender instead. The fast-turning blade on the end of the tool breaks up the ingredients, thickening the soup or stew at the same time. If you want a completely puréed soup, just keep whirling away.

Here are some of our favorite recipes to check out:

**30-Minute Chili Pot (page 20)**

**Summer Tomato Bowl (page 51)**

**Roasted Corn Chowder (page 55)**

**Ham & Vegetable Stew (page 59)**

**Italian Cupboard Stew (page 98)**

**Manhattan Clam Chowder (page 137)**

*Ham & Vegetable Stew, page 59*

*30-Minute Chili Pot, page 20*

*Manhattan Chowder, page 137*

*Garlicky Potato-Leek Soup, page 27*

# Soups
# Every Day

Time for supper! Grab your soup pot, one of our recipes in this chapter, and start stirring. You'll soon be spooning up bowls of soup —fast, flaming hot, and fabulous. But not just any bowl of soup. Ones that taste so rich and flavorful, like they've been simmering for hours. Whisk up a creamy corn bisque, bake an onion soup dripping with melted cheese, and bubble up everyone's favorite of chicken and rice. Or mix up our half-hour chili pot. You'll find these soups are quicker to fix than ever before, thanks to time-saving shortcuts and today's ready-to-use products. Soup has never been so simple, so speedy, so good!

# CHICKEN-TARRAGON SOUP

*Prep* **10 MINUTES**    *Cook* **12 MINUTES**

2     tablespoons butter or margarine

1     cup chopped onion

½     cup sliced celery

1     garlic clove, crushed

2     cans (14½ ounces each) chicken broth

1     can (8 ounces) mixed vegetables

1     can (14 ounces) Italian-style stewed tomatoes

1     cup diced cooked chicken

3     tablespoons chopped fresh parsley

¼     teaspoon dried tarragon, crumbled

*Chicken and tarragon make the perfect match—in no time flat. Add an Italian touch of tomatoes and and some flavor-packed sautéed vegetables. Then just simmer and serve!*

**LET'S BEGIN** Melt the butter in a large saucepan over medium heat. Add the onion, celery, and garlic and cook, stirring, for 6 minutes, or until the onion has softened.

**STIR IT IN** Add the broth, mixed vegetables, tomatoes, chicken, parsley, and tarragon and bring to a boil.

**SIMMER LOW** Reduce the heat. Cover and simmer for 5 minutes, or until the flavors blend.

*Makes 4 servings*

*Per serving: 230 calories, 17g protein, 16g carbohydrates, 10g fat, 5g saturated fat, 48mg cholesterol, 1,034mg sodium*

---

## Cook to Cook

### HOW CAN I MAKE A QUICK BROTH THAT TASTES GOOD?

"I make a *great chicken stock in less than a half hour,* instead of three! Start with a chicken or vegetable broth that comes in an aseptic package. If you can't find one, buy a reduced-sodium broth in a can. And skip the bouillon cubes…they usually have MSG (monosodiumglutamate) with strong salty and onion flavors.

When you're roasting a chicken, *don't throw out the bones.* Cut them up into small pieces, leaving any meat that's on them. Then pop into the freezer. When you need a chicken broth, simmer up some canned broth, dropping in about ½ cup bones per can. Cook for 20 minutes, then strain out the bones, leaving a homemade flavor.

For even more home-cooked flavor, *pick up a pack of soup vegetables* (it's cheap!). It usually has a carrot, a potato, an onion, and sometimes a parsnip. Chop up about 3 cups, sauté them, and toss them into 6 cups of broth. Simmer for 30 minutes, then strain out the veggies. Freeze any extras in ice cube trays for quick flavor-cubes."

# HEARTY CHICKEN & RICE BOWL

*Prep* **15 MINUTES**   *Cook* **36 MINUTES**

| | |
|---|---|
| 1 | cup chopped onion |
| 1 | cup sliced celery |
| 1 | cup sliced carrots |
| ¼ | cup chopped fresh parsley |
| ¾ | cup uncooked long-grain white rice |
| ½ | teaspoon cracked black peppercorns |
| ½ | teaspoon dried thyme |
| 1 | bay leaf |
| 10 | cups chicken broth |
| ¾ | pound boneless, skinless chicken breast halves, cut into ¾-inch chunks |
| 2 | tablespoons lime juice |

*Homemade chicken and rice soup—just like grandma used to serve, but in half the time. If you don't have homemade broth, canned broth works, thanks to all the fresh ingredients in the pot.*

**LET'S BEGIN** Bring all of the ingredients except the chicken and lime juice in a soup pot to a boil over high heat.

**SIMMER LOW** Reduce the heat, cover, and simmer for 20 minutes. Add the chicken and simmer 8 to 10 minutes more, or until the chicken is cooked through.

**SERVE** Remove the bay leaf and stir in the lime juice.

*Makes 8 servings*

*Per serving: 238 calories, 24g protein, 26g carbohydrates, 3g fat, 1g saturated fat, 33mg cholesterol, 1,360mg sodium*

*SuperQuick*
# 30-MINUTE CHILI POT

*Prep* **10 MINUTES**    *Cook* **20 MINUTES**

1    **can (15½ ounces) each: black beans, chickpeas, and red kidney beans**

2    **tablespoons vegetable oil**

1    **large onion, chopped**

2    **medium carrots, chopped**

1    **large green bell pepper**

2    **garlic cloves, minced**

1    **can (28 ounces) diced tomatoes, undrained**

2    **teaspoons hot pepper sauce**

*Here's one of the fastest chili pots around! It all starts with three cans of beans. For variety, try others: pinto, white, or red beans.*

**LET'S BEGIN** Rinse and drain all of the beans. Heat the oil in a large saucepan over medium heat. Add the onion, carrots, green pepper, and garlic. Cook, stirring, for 8 minutes, or until the vegetables have softened.

**STIR IT IN** Add all of the beans and all of the remaining ingredients. Bring to a boil over high heat.

**SIMMER LOW** Reduce the heat to low. Cover and simmer, stirring occasionally, for 12 to 15 minutes to blend the flavors.

> **Makes 6 servings**
>
> *Per serving: 296 calories, 13g protein, 49g carbohydrates, 6g fat, 1g saturated fat, 0mg cholesterol, 1,532mg sodium*

---

*SuperQuick*
# FIERY RICE 'N' BEAN POT

*Prep* **5 MINUTES**    *Cook* **18 MINUTES**

1    **package (1¼ ounces) hot chili seasoning**

2    **cups cooked white rice**

2    **cans (14½ ounces each) pinto beans, undrained**

2    **cups reduced-sodium chicken broth**

1    **can (14½ ounces) stewed tomatoes**

1    **cup chopped scallions**

**Shredded Monterey Jack cheese (optional)**

*This fast-fix rice-and-bean soup is thick and spicy! Have some tortilla chips, a cold salad, and icy drinks ready for action.*

**LET'S BEGIN** Combine all of the ingredients, except the cheese, if using, in a large saucepan.

**SIMMER IT LOW** Bring to a boil. Reduce the heat. Cover and simmer for 15 minutes, or until the flavors blend.

**SERVE** Ladle the soup into bowls and top with Monterey Jack cheese, if desired.

> **Makes 8 servings**
>
> *Per serving: 185 calories, 8g protein, 35g carbohydrates, 1g fat, 0g saturated fat, 1mg cholesterol, 946mg sodium*

*30-Minute Chili Pot*

# TOUCHDOWN CHILI

*Prep* **5 MINUTES**     *Cook* **20 MINUTES**

| | |
|---|---|
| 1 | **can (15 ounces) kidney beans or black beans** |
| 1 | **pound ground beef or ground turkey** |
| 1 | **cup chopped vegetables, such as bell pepper, carrot, and onion** |
| 1 | **can (14½ ounces) diced tomatoes** |
| 1 | **can (8 ounces) tomato sauce** |
| 1 | **package (1¼ ounces) chili seasoning** |
| ½ | **cup shredded Cheddar cheese** |
| ¼ | **cup chopped onion** |

*You won't get past the first down without this quick chili. With chopped veggies, beans, and meat, it's a whole meal in a bowl that kids and adults alike will love.*

**LET'S BEGIN** Drain and rinse the beans. Cook the ground beef and chopped vegetables in a large skillet over medium-high heat until the meat is no longer pink, breaking the meat up with the side of a spoon. Drain off the excess fat.

**SIMMER IT LOW** Stir in the beans, tomatoes, tomato sauce, and chili seasoning and bring to a boil. Reduce the heat. Cover and simmer, stirring occasionally, for 10 minutes or until the flavors blend.

**SERVE** Ladle the soup into bowls and top with the Cheddar and onion.

*Makes 4 servings*

*Per serving: 520 calories, 32g protein, 32g carbohydrates, 29g fat, 12g saturated fat, 100mg cholesterol, 2,046mg sodium*

# GOLDEN-GLOW SOUP

*Prep* **10 MINUTES**    *Cook* **30 MINUTES**

2    medium carrots, peeled and chopped (about 2 cups)

1    medium onion, chopped

1    tablespoon canola oil

1    large sweet potato or yam, peeled and chopped (about 1 cup)

2    cups orange juice

3    cups reduced-sodium chicken broth

Salt and ground black pepper

¼    cup low-fat or nonfat sour cream

¼    cup sliced scallion

*Carrots, sweet potatoes, and orange juice make this sweet purée very filling. No one will ever suspect it's low in fat as well.*

**LET'S BEGIN**  Sauté carrots and onion in the oil in a sauce pot over medium heat for 3 to 4 minutes, or until glazed.

**STIR IT IN**  Add the sweet potatoes, orange juice, and broth and bring to a boil.  Reduce the heat and simmer for 25 to 30 minutes, until the sweet potatoes are tender.

**PURÉE IT SMOOTH**  Purée the soup in a blender or food processor. Return the soup to the pot and season to taste with salt and pepper. Ladle the soup into bowls and top each with a dollop of the sour cream and some of the scallion. Serve hot or refrigerate and serve chilled.

*Makes 4 servings*
*Per serving: 180 calories, 5g protein, 28g carbohydrates, 6g fat, 1g saturated fat, 6mg cholesterol, 513mg sodium*

# CREAMY CORN BISQUE

*Prep* **15 MINUTES**     *Cook* **15 MINUTES**

| | |
|---|---|
| ¾ | pound potatoes, peeled |
| 1 | tablespoon olive oil |
| 1 | large leek (white portion only), rinsed and chopped |
| 2 | carrots, diced |
| ¾ | teaspoon dried thyme |
| ½ | teaspoon dried basil |
| 1 | can (14½ ounces) reduced-sodium chicken broth |
| 1 | can (10¾ ounces) condensed cream of corn soup |
| 1 | cup each: half-and-half and water |
| 1 | cup frozen whole-kernel corn |
| ¼ | teaspoon salt |
| 1 | tablespoon hot pepper sauce |

Red Pepper Cream
(see recipe)

Chopped fresh chives
(optional)

*Make this gorgeous red pepper-crowned corn bisque for company and enjoy the raves. Only you know it's incredibly easy to fix.*

**LET'S BEGIN**  Cut the potatoes into ½-inch chunks (you need 2 cups). Prepare the Red Pepper Cream.

**GET COOKING**  Heat the oil in a large saucepan over medium heat.  Sauté the leek and carrots for 4 minutes, or until just tender. Add the thyme and basil and cook 1 minute more.  Stir in the chicken broth and potatoes. Bring to a boil.

**SIMMER LOW**  Reduce the heat to low. Cover and simmer for 5 minutes, or until the potatoes are just tender. Stir in the corn soup, half-and-half, water, corn, and salt.  Bring to a boil, then reduce the heat and simmer, stirring, for 3 minutes. Stir in the hot pepper sauce. Ladle the soup into bowls. Top each with a dollop of red-pepper cream and decoratively swirl it into the soup. Sprinkle with chives, if desired.

## RED PEPPER CREAM

*Purée 1 jar (7 ounces) drained roasted red peppers, 3 tablespoons sour cream, and 2 tablespoons hot pepper sauce in a food processor or blender.*

*Makes 4 servings*

*Per serving: 309 calories, 8g protein, 38g carbohydrates, 15g fat, 7g saturated fat, 28mg cholesterol, 1,645mg sodium*

# BROCCOLI-CHEDDAR SOUP AMANDINE

*Prep* **15 MINUTES**     *Cook* **30 MINUTES**

*Toast the almonds in a dry skillet over medium-high heat. Keep tossing until they're lightly golden. Then make this easy elegant soup from cans of chicken broth.*

| | |
|---|---|
| ¾ | cup blanched slivered almonds, toasted |
| 2 | tablespoons butter or margarine |
| 2 | large onions, thinly sliced (about 2 cups) |
| 1 | bunch broccoli, chopped (about 4 cups) |
| 1 | large potato, peeled and cubed |
| 2 | cans (14½ ounces each) chicken broth |
| ½ | teaspoon dried thyme |
| ½ | cup milk |
| 1¼ | cups shredded Cheddar cheese (about 5 ounces) |

**LET'S BEGIN** Finely grind ½ cup of the almonds in a food processor or blender. Melt the butter in a large saucepan over medium-high heat. Sauté the onions for 5 minutes, or until softened and lightly browned. Stir in the broccoli, potato, broth, and thyme. Reduce the heat. Cover and simmer for 20 minutes, or until the potatoes and broccoli are tender.

**PROCESS IT SMOOTH** Purée the soup in a food processor or blender. Return the purée to the pot. Stir in the milk and heat just to boiling. Remove from the heat and whisk in 1 cup of the Cheddar until smooth. Whisk in the ground almonds.

**SERVE** Ladle the soup into bowls and garnish with the remaining ¼ cup almonds and ¼ cup Cheddar.

**Makes 4 to 6 servings**

*Per serving: 496 calories, 24g protein, 27g carbohydrates, 34g fat, 13g saturated fat, 58mg cholesterol, 985mg sodium*

---

## On the Menu

*Enjoy an evening in a Paris bistro with this quick and simple soup meal.*

---

Broccoli-Cheddar Soup Amandine

Warm Baguette with Parsley-Garlic Butter

Sliced Tomato Salad with White Wine Vinaigrette

Fresh Raspberries with Sweet Whipped Cream

French-roast Coffee

# GARLICKY POTATO-LEEK SOUP

*Prep* **20 MINUTES**    *Cook* **17 MINUTES**

1½  pounds Yukon Gold potatoes, peeled and cut into ½-inch cubes

2  medium leeks, white part only, trimmed, sliced, and rinsed

2  medium carrots, peeled and diced

2  garlic cloves, minced

1  carton (32 ounces) chicken broth

1  cup light cream or half-and-half

1  cup loosely packed fresh baby spinach

*Leeks are notorious for being very sandy between the layers. Clean them fast by throwing the slices into a bowl of cold water and swishing them around several times.*

**LET'S BEGIN** Combine the first 5 ingredients in a medium saucepan and bring to a boil over high heat.

**SIMMER LOW** Reduce the heat and simmer for 10 minutes, or until the vegetables are tender.

**COOK IT QUICK** Stir in the cream and spinach and cook for 3 minutes, or until the soup is heated through and the spinach has wilted.

*Makes 6 servings*

*Per serving: 223 calories, 5g protein, 31g carbohydrates, 9g fat, 5g saturated fat, 26mg cholesterol, 671mg sodium*

---

## Cooking Basics

### THE BEST ONIONS FOR THE SOUP POT

**FRESH IS FAST & SWEET**

Onions come two ways: "fresh and sweet" and "hot and dry, as storage onions." The fresh ones—such as leeks, scallions, Vidalia, Maui, Georgia, Walla Walla, and Texas Super Sweets—have a low sulphur content (that's what makes you cry when chopping). They're perfect for tossing into soups and stews…their sweet fragrance flavors soups fast.

**LOVE THOSE LEEKS!**

When choosing onions for soups and stews, you can't beat leeks! They have that prized flavor that permeates the pot, giving it a mild pleasing onion taste— not strong and heavy like their dried cousins. Pick smaller leeks for the sweetest flavor. The more delicate scallions work great in the pot too, especially in creamed soups.

**HOT & DRIED**

Storage onions, with their hot intense flavor, go a long way in the soup pot (so use less). Large yellow Spanish onions give that familiar strong flavor…red Spanish onions, a hotter but slightly sweet taste…the Texas whites, the mildest flavor of all the storage onions. Tiny shallots add both the flavors of garlic and onion to the soup pot.

# ONION SOUP WITH ROASTED SUNFLOWER KERNELS

*Prep* **15 MINUTES**     *Bake/Cook* **15 MINUTES**

2    tablespoons butter or margarine

3    large onions, thinly sliced

2    cups beef broth

1    cup dry white wine

½    teaspoon caraway seeds

Ground black pepper

8    slices French bread

⅓    cup roasted sunflower kernels

1    cup shredded Gruyère or Swiss cheese

*Make this quick-but-savory onion soup with its cap of melted cheese even yummier with a sprinkle of crunchy sunflower kernels.*

**LET'S BEGIN**  Preheat the oven to 350°F. Melt the butter in a heavy skillet over medium heat. Add the onions and cook for 6 minutes, or until softened. Add the beef broth, wine, and caraway seeds, and season with pepper. Simmer for 5 to 10 minutes.

**SERVE**  Ladle the soup into 4 ovenproof soup bowls. Place 2 slices of bread on top of the soup in each bowl. Sprinkle with the sunflower kernels and cheese. Bake until the cheese has melted and is golden brown. For crusty tops, place the soup bowls under the broiler for several minutes.

*Makes 4 servings*

*Per serving: 476 calories, 19g protein, 38g carbohydrates, 24g fat, 11g saturated fat, 52mg cholesterol, 874mg sodium*

*SuperQuick*
# SHERRIED PUMPKIN SOUP
*Prep* **10 MINUTES**     *Cook* **20 MINUTES**

*Cut 15 minutes of cook time by precooking the potato cubes in the microwave. Sprinkle them with a little water, cover, and microwave for 3 minutes on High. Toss them in with the pumpkin.*

| | |
|---|---|
| 1 | large onion, chopped (about 1 cup) |
| 1 | tablespoon vegetable oil |
| 4 | cups reduced-sodium chicken broth |
| 1 | medium all-purpose potato, peeled and diced |
| 1 | can (15 ounces) unsweetened pumpkin purée |
| ¼ | cup dry sherry |
| ¼ | teaspoon ground nutmeg |
| 1 | cup plain yogurt |
| | Salt and ground black pepper |
| | Toasted pumpkin seeds (optional) |

**LET'S BEGIN** Heat the oil in a large sauce pot over medium heat. Sauté the onion for 3 minutes. Add the broth and bring to a boil. Add the potato. Reduce the heat and simmer for 15 minutes, or until the potato is almost tender. Stir in the pumpkin purée, sherry, and nutmeg and bring to a boil.

**PROCESS IT SMOOTH** Purée the mixture in a food processor or blender. Return to the pot and bring to a simmer. Transfer ¼ cup of the soup to a bowl, whisk in the yogurt, then ¾ cup more soup. Return to soup pot and heat through (do not let boil or it will curdle). Season with salt and pepper. Serve warm or cold. Garnish with pumpkin seeds, if you wish.

*Makes 5 servings*

*Per serving: 148 calories, 7g protein, 19g carbohydrates, 5g fat, 1g saturated fat, 6mg cholesterol, 531mg sodium*

## Microwave in Minutes

### SPEEDING UP THE SOUP POT

Put your microwave to work to cut simmering time of soups and stews—by precooking some of the longer-cooking ingredients in your microwave first.

***Poach chicken breasts in minutes in the microwave,*** then just toss them into the soup or stew the last few minutes of cooking. Here's how: Place 2 boneless, skinless breast halves on a microwavable glass pie plate. Season with salt and pepper and drizzle with 1 tablespoon of broth, water, or wine. Cover with a paper towel and cook on High for 3 to 4 minutes, turning over once. Let stand for 2 minutes.

***Jump-start "tough" veggies in the microwave.*** Broccoli, carrots, and even celery cook much faster in the stew pot if microwaved first. Spread in a single layer on a microwavable glass pie plate, pointing the toughest parts, such as the broccoli stems, toward the edge. Sprinkle with a little broth or wine and cook on High for 3 minutes, then add to the stew pot.

***Steam potato chunks*** for 3 minutes on High, then add to the stew pot.

# SWEET POTATO & YOGURT SOUP

*Prep* **15 MINUTES**     *Cook* **30 MINUTES**

| | |
|---|---|
| 1 | tablespoon vegetable oil |
| 1 | large onion, chopped (about 2 cups) |
| 2 | medium sweet potatoes, peeled and diced (about 2 cups) |
| 1 | medium baking potato, peeled and diced (about 1 cup) |
| 4 | cups reduced-sodium chicken broth |
| 2 | cups plain yogurt |

Salt and ground black pepper

| | |
|---|---|
| 2 | tablespoons chopped fresh chives |

*Creamy sweet potato and yogurt soup is oh so satisfying on a cold winter day. If you don't have any chives, slice green onion tops.*

**LET'S BEGIN** Heat the oil in a medium saucepan over medium heat. Add the onion and cook, stirring, for 3 to 4 minutes. Add all the potatoes and broth and bring to a boil.

**SIMMER LOW** Reduce the heat and simmer for 25 minutes, or until the potatoes are very tender and the flavors blend.

**PROCESS IT SMOOTH** Purée the soup in a food processor or blender and transfer to a large bowl. Whisk in the yogurt and season to taste with salt and pepper. Ladle the soup into bowls and sprinkle with chives.

*Makes 8 servings*

*Per serving: 250 calories, 10g protein, 36g carbohydrates, 8g fat, 3g saturated fat, 16mg cholesterol, 695mg sodium*

---

## Food Facts

### "GOOD FOR YOU" SWEET-POTATO SOUPS

**GO FOR THE ORANGE!**
The deep orange color in sweet potatoes doesn't just make them pretty—it makes them good for you, too. It's beta-carotene, the compound our bodies convert into vitamin A. This vitamin helps our eyes adjust easily to the dark. Plus it keeps the skin healthy, thus helping to prevent infections. One serving of our Sweet Potato & Yogurt Soup gives you 100 percent of the Daily Value (DV) of vitamin A!

**DON'T FORGET CALCIUM**
Yogurt (a fermented milk product) is rich in calcium, playing a crucial part in keeping our bones and teeth healthy. One cup of yogurt provides 45 percent of the DV for calcium.

*BLT Bowl*

*Summer Tomato Bowl, page 51*

# Fast & Fresh

Every spoonful from the soup recipes here bursts with fresh ingredients and homegrown flavors. And the best part: they're fast to fix, most can be made in a half hour or less. Pick one of our fresh vegetable soups and discover how to chop up veggies even faster with the help of today's handy equipment. Whisk up a cheesy broccoli bowl, bubble up a hearty tortellini pot, whirl up a fresh zucchini soup with a zesty pesto, or simmer up a savory seafood stew. Enjoy the convenience of mixing up a cold soup one day, then refrigerate to serve at a moment's notice the next. You'll find it's easier and quicker than you thought to ladle up a fresh homemade soup, even on the spur of the moment.

# TURKEY VEGETABLE SOUP

*Prep* **10 MINUTES**    *Cook* **15 MINUTES**

*Make an easy turkey broth with the bones from the Thanksgiving bird. Place the carcass in a pot, cover with cold water, and simmer for 2 hours (no covering, please). For extra flavor, toss in some sliced onion, carrots, and celery—plus fresh thyme, if you like.*

| | |
|---|---|
| 1 | tablespoon vegetable oil |
| 3 | large celery ribs, diced |
| 2 | large carrots, peeled and diced |
| 1 | large onion, diced |
| 2 | cups diced cooked turkey |
| 1 | can (15 ounces) cream-style corn |
| 3½ | cups homemade turkey broth or reduced-sodium chicken broth |
| ¼ | cup chopped fresh parsley |
| 1¾ | teaspoons salt |
| 1 | teaspoon hot pepper sauce |
| ½ | cup small bow-tie pasta or egg noodles |

**LET'S BEGIN** Heat the oil in a medium saucepan over medium heat. Add the celery, carrots, and onion and cook, stirring occasionally, for 5 minutes, or until crisp-tender.

**STIR IT IN** Add all of the remaining ingredients. Bring to a boil.

**SIMMER SLOW** Reduce the heat. Cover and simmer, stirring a few times, for 10 to 15 minutes, until pasta is tender.

*Makes 4 servings*

*Per serving: 370 calories, 30g protein, 47g carbohydrates, 8g fat, 2g saturated fat, 53mg cholesterol, 1,978mg sodium*

---

### Cooking Basics

#### SKIMMING AWAY FOAM & FAT FAST

**CLEAR IS BEST**

While soups and stocks (especially those with meat and bones) simmer in the pot, foam and fat rise to the top. They're filled with impurities and unwanted extra fat. Skim them away periodically, using a mesh skimmer or spoon.

**LETTUCE IS NOT JUST FOR EATING**

To remove more fat, chill the soup and scoop off the congealed layer of fat that forms. If there's no time to chill, remove soup from the heat and blot surface with a large cold lettuce leaf. Excess fat floating on the top of the soup will cling to the cold leaf, leaving stock crystal-clear.

**PAPER CHASE**

Another way to blot off the fat fast is with a paper towel, folded in half. Pull it across the top of the stock bringing the fat with it.

# CREAMY VEGETABLE CUP

*Prep* **8 MINUTES**      *Cook* **22 MINUTES**

| | |
|---|---|
| 1 | large onion, chopped (1 cup) |
| 1 | tablespoon olive oil |
| 4 | cups low-sodium chicken broth |
| 1½ | cups carrot chunks |
| 1½ | cups peeled, diced potato |
| 1½ | cups plain yogurt |
| 1 | tablespoon honey |

**Salt and ground black pepper**

| | |
|---|---|
| ¼ | cup chopped chives |

*Here's a fast way to get your vegetables. Purée fresh, cooked vegetables, then whisk in a creamy yogurt. Good—and good for you!*

**LET'S BEGIN** Sauté the onion in the oil in a saucepot for 2 minutes over medium-high heat. Add the broth, carrots, and potato and cook for 20 minute. Remove from heat and cool.

**PROCESS IT SMOOTH** Purée the mixture until smooth in a blender or food processor and return to saucepan. Bring the soup to a simmer over medium heat.

**MIX & SERVE** Place 1 cup of the yogurt in a small bowl and gradually blend in 1 cup of soup. Return to pot. Stir in the honey, salt, and pepper. (Don't let it boil!) Serve the soup warm or cold with the remaining yogurt and chives on top.

> *Makes 4 servings*
>
> *Per serving: 228 calories, 9g protein, 30g carbohydrates, 9g fat, 3g saturated fat, 17mg cholesterol, 275mg sodium*

# MAC & VEGETABLE POT

*Prep* **10 MINUTES**      *Cook* **18 MINUTES**

| | |
|---|---|
| 4 | cans (14½ ounces each) low-sodium chicken broth |
| 1 | cup each: chopped red pepper, carrots & celery |
| 1 | large onion, sliced |
| 2 | garlic cloves, minced |
| 1 | teaspoon dried basil |
| ¼ | teaspoon ground pepper |
| 1 | cup uncooked spiral macaroni |
| ½ | cup frozen corn kernels |

*Another fast way to serve up supper…this time in a simple broth with a bouquet of garden vegetables and pasta spirals.*

**LET'S BEGIN** Combine all of the ingredients except the macaroni and corn in a large saucepan and bring to a boil over medium-high heat.

**SIMMER & STIR** Add the macaroni and simmer for 10 minutes. Stir in the corn and cook for 5 minutes more, the or the until macaroni is done.

> *Makes 8 servings*
>
> *Per serving: 110 calories, 6g protein, 19g carbohydrates, 2g fat, 1g saturated fat, 3mg cholesterol, 110mg sodium*

*SuperQuick*
# GARDEN VEGETABLE SOUP
*Prep* **15 MINUTES**      *Cook* **10 MINUTES**

¾  cup whole natural almonds

1  onion, cut into thin wedges

½  cup sliced celery

1  green pepper, cut into slivers

2  tablespoons almond or polyunsaturated oil

1  can (13¾ ounces) chicken broth or stock

½  cup dry white wine

1  garlic clove, minced

1  teaspoon basil, crumbled

½  teaspoon oregano

⅛  teaspoon ground pepper

1  medium tomato, cut into small chunks

*Make this easy veggie soup with either chicken or vegetable broth. As you chop the onion, celery, and pepper, double the amounts and freeze half. Next time, there's no chopping—just cooking.*

**LET'S BEGIN** Quickly toast the almonds in a skillet over low heat for 2 minutes or until golden, tossing constantly. Pulse almonds in a food processor until coarsely chopped.

**INTO THE PAN** Coat a large saucepot with cooking spray and place over medium heat. Sauté the onion, celery, and green pepper for 5 minutes, or until tender-crisp.

**MIX & SERVE** Mix in the broth, wine, garlic, basil, oregano, and pepper and heat through. Add the tomato and heat through. Ladle the soup into bowls. Spoon the almonds into the center of each bowl.

*Makes 4 servings*

*Per serving: 300 calories, 9g protein, 14g carbohydrates, 22g fat, 2g saturated fat, 0mg cholesterol, 330mg sodium*

---

## Food Facts

### ALMONDS—A HEART-HEALTHY NUT

Simmer up a pot of this Garden Vegetable Soup, that's chock full of vegetables and almonds. And be good to your heart! According to the Food & Drug Association, scientific evidence suggests that eating 1½ ounces of most nuts, such as almonds, as part of a diet low in saturated fat and cholesterol, may reduce the risk of heart disease. They are high in monounsaturated fats, which lower LDLs (the bad cholesterol) and raise HDLs (the good cholesterol).

# BROCCOLI-CHEESE BOWL
*Prep* **10 MINUTES**     *Cook* **15 MINUTES**

| | |
|---|---|
| 3 | cups broccoli florets, fresh or frozen & thawed |
| 1 | tablespoon butter or margarine |
| 1 | medium onion, chopped |
| 1 | tablespoon all-purpose flour |
| 1 | teaspoon salt |
| 3 | cups soy milk |
| 2 | teaspoons cornstarch |
| 6 | ounces shredded Cheddar cheese |

Popped corn (optional)

*Take the "crunch" out of the broccoli by microwaving it a minute on High. Drain, then toss into the pot during the last two minutes.*

**LET'S BEGIN** Chop the broccoli. Melt butter in a sauce pot over medium heat. Add the onion, flour, and salt and sauté for 3 minutes. Whisk together the milk and cornstarch in a small bowl until smooth, then stir into the onion mixture.

**BUBBLE & STIR** Cook the soup, stirring frequently, for 5 to 7 minutes, or until thick and bubbly. Stir in the cheese and cook for 3 to 5 minutes more, or until cheese melts. Add broccoli and stir until hot. Top with popped corn, if you wish.

*Makes 5 servings*

*Per serving: 240 calories, 14g protein, 10g carbohydrates, 17g fat, 9g saturated fat, 42mg cholesterol, 734mg sodium*

## On the Menu

*Transform your dining room into a trendy café with this quick heart-healthy menu.*

*Broccoli-Cheese Bowl*

*Mixed Baby Lettuce with Sunflower Seeds*

*Whole-Grain Rolls & Honey*

*Rice Pudding with Apricots*

# CARROT SOUP
*Prep* **10 MINUTES**    *Cook* **20 MINUTES**

1    **pound carrots, peeled and thinly sliced**

1    **onion, chopped**

2    **cups chicken broth**

2    **tablespoons honey**

1    **cup milk or half-and-half**

**Sour cream or plain yogurt, as needed**

**Ground nutmeg**

**Minced chives**

*To save cook time and chopping, substitute a 20-ounce package of frozen sliced carrots for the fresh. After adding the milk, watch carefully and don't let the soup boil. It may lose its creaminess.*

**LET'S BEGIN** Combine the carrots, onion and chicken broth in a sauce pot. Cover and simmer for about 15 minutes, or until the carrots are tender.

**PROCESS SMOOTH** Purée the mixture in a food processor or blender until smooth. Return to sauce pot.

**SIMMER IT LOW** Whisk in the honey and milk and heat until steaming. Serve hot or cold with a dollop of sour cream. Sprinkle with nutmeg and garnish with chives.

*Makes 6 servings*

*Per serving: 102 calories, 4g protein, 18g carbohydrates, 2g fat, 1g saturated fat, 6mg cholesterol, 306mg sodium*

---

## Cooking Basics

### SAVE TIME WITH THE RIGHT TOOLS

The right tools make all the difference in fast-starting the soup pot. Try one of the chopping machines on the market to help you get ingredients into the soup pot in a quarter of the time.

**The fancy professional stainless steel mandoline from France** is a hand-operated cutting machine used by professional chefs.

They'll perfect for slicing firm fruits and vegetables uniformly, whatever thickness you wish. But they're expensive!

**The new sturdy plastic mandolines,** imported from Japan and Germany, have razor-sharp blades that slice almost as well as the more expensive French machines at only about one-fourth the cost.

**For the most versatile chopping machine of them all,** choose the top of the line, versatile food processors (if your budget can take it!). They chop, blend, purée, and even make doughs. You can use various slicing blades to match whatever slicing job you have. The price varies with size of processor bowl, speeds, and attachments.

# HEARTY TORTELLINI POT

*Prep* **15 MINUTES**     *Cook* **10 MINUTES**

| | |
|---|---|
| 2 | **tablespoons olive oil** |
| 1 | **small red onion, chopped** |
| 2 | **medium carrots, chopped** |
| 2 | **celery ribs, thinly sliced** |
| 1 | **small zucchini, chopped** |
| 2 | **plum tomatoes, chopped** |
| 2 | **garlic cloves, minced** |
| 2 | **cans (14½ ounces each) chicken broth** |
| ½ | **cup water** |
| 1 | **can (15 to 19 ounces) red kidney beans, rinsed and drained** |
| 2 | **tablespoons Worcestershire sauce** |
| 1 | **package (9 ounces) refrigerated fresh tortellini pasta** |

*Cook as they do in Italy, with the freshest vegetables and delicious pasta. Make this hearty soup superquick with the help of your chopping machine and ready-made products such as fresh tortellini.*

**LET'S BEGIN** Heat the oil in a 6-quart saucepot or Dutch oven over medium-high heat. Add the onion, carrots, celery, zucchini, tomatoes, and garlic. Cook for 5 minutes, or until the vegetables are crisp-tender, stirring frequently.

**BUBBLE & STIR** Add the broth, water, beans, and Worcestershire sauce. Bring the soup to a boil.

**STIR IT IN** Stir in the pasta and return the soup to a boil. Cook for 5 minutes, or until the pasta is tender, stirring occasionally. Serve with crusty bread and grated Parmesan cheese, if you like.

*Makes 4 servings*

*Per serving: 422 calories, 21g protein, 57g carbohydrates, 13g fat, 3g saturated fat, 34mg cholesterol, 1,383mg sodium*

---

## Food Facts

### THE LEGEND OF TORTELLINI

The Emilia-Romagna region in the heart of Italy has been famous for its freshly made Bologna pasta since the 14th century. The most prized pasta of them all is the tortellini. Legend claims it began back in the days when gods still walked the earth. Tortellini was created one night when Zeus and Venus visited an inn in Bologna. The innkeeper was so dazzled by Venus' beauty that he worked through the night in his kitchen to make something in her honor. He finally emerged at dawn with a new pasta, which he named *Tortellini*. Its shape was modeled after the goddess' navel. Centuries later, tortellini's nickname in Bologna, even in the "finest of circles," is *sacred navels*.

# ZUCCHINI–PESTO SOUP
*Prep* **15 MINUTES**     *Cook* **15 MINUTES**

**Almond Pesto (see recipe)**

¼     **cup butter**

½     **cup chopped onion**

6     **cups sliced zucchini**

2     **cans (10¾ ounces each) condensed chicken broth**

1     **teaspoon seasoned salt**

½     **teaspoon dried thyme, crumbled**

¼     **teaspoon white pepper**

2     **cups heavy cream**

*Choose zucchini carefully for this soup. Pick out small ones (not over 8 inches long) with taut skin and no blemishes.*

**LET'S BEGIN** Make the pesto. Melt the butter in a soup pot over medium heat. Stir in the onion and cook for 5 minutes, or until soft. Add the zucchini and sauté 3 minutes more. Stir in the broth, salt, thyme, and white pepper and heat through.

**PROCESS IT SMOOTH** Purée the zucchini mixture in a food processor or blender and return to pot with the heavy cream. Heat slowly (don't let it boil!). Ladle into individual soup bowls and top each with 1 tablespoon of pesto.

## ALMOND PESTO
*Mix together one 4-ounce container of frozen pesto (thawed), ½ cup diced roasted almonds, ⅓ cup grated Parmesan cheese, ¼ cup olive, oil, 1 tablespoon chopped fresh parsley, and 1 tablespoon fresh lemon juice.*

*Makes 6 servings*

*Per serving: 473 calories, 7g protein, 10g carbohydrates, 47g fat, 25g saturated fat, 137mg cholesterol, 1,080mg sodium*

---

### Cook to Cook

#### WHAT CAN I DO WITH PESTO OTHER THAN TOSS IT WITH PASTA?

"*I spread focaccia with pesto,* sprinkle with basil and serve hot with soups.

*I use pesto to spice up pasta salads.* One of my favorites is tossing bow-tie pasta with cooked fresh green peas, tuna, and a vinaigrette dressing.

*Garnish soups with a dollop of pesto.* It's great on vegetable chicken, potato, even tomato soups.

*Pesto makes a great sandwich spread*—especially on fresh tomato and mozzarella ones on country bread.

Pesto is *perfect for topping broiled fish or seafood stews.*

*Spread pesto on chicken breasts,* between the skin and the meat, before baking.

I turn *cooked rice into a pilaf* by tossing it with pesto."

# ASPARAGUS-LEMON SOUP

*Prep* **10 MINUTES**    *Cook* **15 MINUTES**

| | |
|---|---|
| 1 | pound fresh asparagus, trimmed and chopped |
| 1 | cup chopped celery |
| 3 | cups chicken broth |
| ½ | teaspoon grated lemon peel |
| 2 | tablespoons fresh lemon juice |
| 1/16 | teaspoon white pepper |
| ½ | cup whipping cream |

*The elegant asparagus cooks and whirls up fast into a homemade soup. Make a double batch: serve some hot, the rest cold.*

**LET'S BEGIN** Bring the first 3 ingredients to a boil in a saucepot over high heat. Reduce the heat to low and simmer for 10 minutes. Cool slightly.

**PROCESS IT SMOOTH** Process the asparagus mixture until smooth in a food processor or blender. Return the soup to the saucepot and stir in the remaining ingredients. Heat the soup until warm (do not boil). Serve hot or cold.

> *Makes 5 servings*
>
> *Per serving: 133 calories, 6g protein, 7g carbohydrates, 10g fat, 6g saturated fat, 33mg cholesterol, 497mg sodium*

# CREAMY SQUASH SOUP

*Prep* **10 MINUTES**    *Cook* **20 MINUTES**

| | |
|---|---|
| 2 | butternut squash (about 4 pounds), peeled, seeded, and cut into small chunks (8 cups) |
| 1 | cup chopped carrots |
| 2 | cans (14½ ounces each) chicken broth |
| 1 | cup water |
| ½ | teaspoon ground pepper |
| 1/8 | teaspoon ground nutmeg |
| ½ | cup sour cream |

*When buying butternut squash for this soup, look for heavy squash with a smooth, hard skin. Cut into small chunks so it cooks fast.*

**LET'S BEGIN** Bring the squash, carrots, broth, and water to a boil in a soup pot over medium-high heat. Reduce the heat. Cover, and simmer for 10 minutes or until vegetables are tender.

**PROCESS IT SMOOTH** Process the squash mixture in a food processor or blender until smooth, working in batches if necessary. Return soup to the pot. Stir in pepper and nutmeg.

**MIX & BLEND** Stir the soup over low heat until hot. Place the sour cream in a small bowl. Blend in about 1 cup of the hot soup, then return mixture to pot and stir. Ladle into bowls.

> *Makes 6 servings*
>
> *Per serving: 150 calories, 5g protein, 25g carbohydrates, 4g fat, 2g saturated fat, 7mg cholesterol, 460mg sodium*

Asparagus-Lemon Soup

# TROPICAL SEAFOOD STEW

*Prep* **15 MINUTES**   *Marinate* **15 MINUTES**   *Cook* **10 MINUTES**

1   **pound orange roughy fillet (or other mild white fish)**

½   **pound large shrimp, peeled and deveined**

½   **cup lemon pepper marinade**

1   **tablespoon vegetable oil**

¼   **cup chopped green bell pepper**

½   **cup chopped onion**

3   **plum tomatoes, chopped**

¼   **cup milk or coconut milk**

**Cooked rice (optional)**

**Chopped cilantro (optional)**

*Substitute flounder, fluke, or sole for the orange roughy. To save time, buy small shrimp already peeled and deveined.*

**LET'S BEGIN** Cut the fillet into 1-inch pieces. Place the fish and shrimp in a resealable plastic bag. Add half of the marinade, turn to coat, and refrigerate for 15 minutes. Set aside the remaining marinade.

**IN THE PAN** Heat the oil in a medium saucepan. Sauté the bell pepper, onion, and tomatoes for 5 minutes. Add the fish and shrimp, discarding any marinade left in the bag.

**STIR IT IN** Cook, stirring occasionally, for 3 minutes, or until the shrimp turn pink and the fish flakes easily with a fork. Stir in the milk and remove the pan from the heat. Serve over rice and garnish with cilantro, if you like.

*Makes 6 servings*

*Per serving: 145 calories, 20g protein, 7g carbohydrates, 4g fat, 1g saturated fat, 74mg cholesterol, 368mg sodium*

---

## Time Savers

### BUYING THE RIGHT SHRIMP

When using shrimp in a soup pot or stew, there are several factors to consider at the fish counter: the size, whether to buy shrimp peeled or unpeeled, cooked or raw. On the average, you'll save at least a half hour of cleaning and boiling time per pound by buying shrimp already shelled, deveined, and precooked. They're ready to drop right into the soup pot a minute or two toward the end of the cooking (but expect to pay more for the convenience!). Peel off the shell and tail and cut out the mud vein along the back.

For a few dollars less per pound, purchase raw shrimp still in the shell. Peel off the shell and tail, then cut out the mud vein that runs along the back.

The count makes a difference. It tells you how many shrimp come in a pound. The higher the count, the more shrimp. The more time you'll spend cleaning them. Medium shrimp come 25 to 30 per pound (fine for soups and stews); large shrimp, 18 to 22 per pound (great for soups); jumbo shrimp, 10 to 12 per pound (save them for scampi).

# SHRIMP GAZPACHO

*Prep* **15 MINUTES**    *Chill* **10 MINUTES**

½    pound medium shrimp, cooked

½    cup chopped onion

½    cup finely chopped green bell pepper

2    cans (14½ ounces each) diced tomatoes, undrained

1    teaspoon dried thyme

1    teaspoon dried tarragon

¼    teaspoon cayenne pepper

French bread (optional)

*This elegant gazpacho comes together in minutes, especially if you buy the shrimp already cooked. Put aside four of the nicest shrimp and use them as a garnish.*

**LET'S BEGIN** Remove the tails from the shrimp if necessary. Rinse the shrimp in a colander under cold water, drain, and place in a large bowl.

**STIR IT IN** Add all of the remaining ingredients except the bread.

**CHILL IT** Cover and chill for at least 10 minutes. Serve the soup with French bread, if you like.

*Makes 4 servings*

*Per serving: 115 calories, 14g protein, 11g carbohydrates, 1g fat, 0g saturated fat, 86mg cholesterol, 746mg sodium*

# AVOCADO-ORANGE CUP

*Prep* **10 MINUTES**    *Chill* **15 MINUTES**

2    large ripe avocados

1    cup fresh orange juice

1    cup plain yogurt

½    teaspoon hot pepper sauce

¼    teaspoon salt

Orange slices

*Here's a fast-to-fix appetizer soup that's perfect for a spicy Tex-Mex supper. Another night, add some cooked chicken and make a meal.*

**LET'S BEGIN** Peel and pit the avocados. Process with the orange juice in a food processor or blender until blended.

**PROCESS SMOOTH** Add the yogurt, hot pepper sauce, and salt. Process until smooth.

**CHILL IT** Refrigerate the soup for 15 minutes, or until ready to serve. Garnish with the orange slices.

*Makes 4 servings*

*Per serving: 268 calories, 5g protein, 20g carbohydrates, 21g fat, 4g saturated fat, 8mg cholesterol, 191mg sodium*

# ZESTY GREEN GAZPACHO

*Prep* **15 MINUTES**      *Chill* **15 MINUTES**

| | |
|---|---|
| 3 | scallions |
| 2 | ribs celery |
| 1 | medium cucumber |
| 1 | green bell pepper |
| 1 | cup green seedless grapes |
| ¼ | cup loosely packed cilantro leaves |
| 2 | tablespoons lime juice |
| 1 | tablespoon green pepper sauce |
| ¼ | teaspoon salt |
| 1 | cup white grape juice |

*Whirl up this beautiful emerald-green gazpacho in minutes on a hot summer day. Substitute parsley for the cilantro, if you wish.*

**LET'S BEGIN** Cut the scallions in half. Cut the celery into large chunks. Peel and seed the cucumber and cut into large chunks. Cut the bell pepper into large pieces.

**PROCESS** Place all the ingredients except the grape juice in a food processor and pulse just to combine (do not purée). Pour the grape juice through the feed tube and pulse enough just to combine the ingredients.

**CHILL** Refrigerate for 15 minutes, or until ready to serve.

*Makes 4 servings*

*Per serving: 98 calories, 2g protein, 24g carbohydrates, 0g fat, 0g saturated fat, 0mg cholesterol, 175mg sodium*

# GARDEN-FRESH RED GAZPACHO

*Prep* **30 MINUTES**    *Chill* **1 HOUR**

| | |
|---|---|
| 5 | large tomatoes (about 2½ pounds) |
| 1 | large cucumber, peeled and seeded |
| 2 | large bell peppers (1 green, 1 red) |
| 2 | scallions, sliced |
| 1 | large red onion |
| 3 | garlic cloves |
| 2 | tablespoons minced fresh basil leaves |
| ¼ | cup hot pepper sauce |
| ¼ | cup red wine vinegar |
| 3 | tablespoons olive oil |
| 1 | teaspoon salt |

*Make this soup look gorgeous by hand-chopping the vegetables that garnish the bowls right before serving. The soup itself whirls up fast in the food processor.*

**LET'S BEGIN** Coarsely chop 1 tomato, ½ cucumber, ½ each green and red bell peppers, and the scallions. Set aside.

**PROCESS SMOOTH** Place the remaining vegetables and all other ingredients in the food processor or blender. Cover and process until smooth, adding in batches if necessary. Transfer soup to a large glass bowl.

**CHILL & SERVE** Set aside ½ cup of the chopped vegetables for garnish. Stir the rest into the soup. Cover and refrigerate soup for at least 1 hour before serving. Garnish with the reserved vegetables.

*Makes 6 servings*

*Per serving: 140 calories, 3g protein, 17g carbohydrates, 8g fat, 1g saturated fat, 0mg cholesterol, 473mg sodium*

## Cooking Basics

### FLAVORING UP THE SOUP POT WITH A BOUQUET GARNI

Take a tip from the French and add flavor to your soup pot with a *bouquet garni*. Traditionally, it's a bundle or pouch of herbs for dropping into a hot soup as it simmers…or a cold soup as it chills.

**BUNDLE UP FRESH HERBS**
Collect the classic combination: fresh parsley, a few fresh thyme sprigs, and one or two fresh bay leaves. Tie with string and drop right into the pot. If you're making a vegetable soup, substitute fresh basil leaves for the bay.

**WRAP UP DRIED HERBS**
To use dried herbs, wrap them up in a square of cheesecloth (double the layers). Add a clove of garlic for

chicken soups…some fresh dill for a seafood pot. Tie the bundle with string, leaving a long enough end to attach to the pot handle (makes it easy to remove the bouquet from the pot). Be sure the string doesn't reach the heating element.

*Summer Tomato Bowl*

# SUMMER TOMATO BOWL

*Prep* **20 MINUTES**     *Chill* **1 HOUR**

| | |
|---|---|
| 4 | cups fresh tomatoes |
| 2 | large cucumbers |
| 1 | large green bell pepper |
| 1 | large onion, finely chopped |
| 1 | garlic clove, finely chopped |
| 1 | jar (46 ounces) low-sodium vegetable juice |
| 2 | tablespoons lemon juice |
| 1 | tablespoon balsamic vinegar |
| 1 | teaspoon Worcestershire sauce |

*If you chop the fresh tomatoes very finely, you can skip peeling them and save a lot of time. Or substitute a 28-ounce can of peeled Italian tomatoes for the fresh tomatoes.*

**LET'S BEGIN** Peel, seed, and chop the tomatoes and cucumbers and place in a large bowl. Seed and chop the bell pepper and add to the bowl.

**MIX IT UP** Stir in all of the remaining ingredients.

**CHILL** Cover and refrigerate until well chilled.

*Makes 8 servings*

*Per serving: 87 calories, 3g protein, 18g carbohydrates, 0g fat, 0g saturated fat, 0mg cholesterol, 116mg sodium*

*SuperQuick*

# CREAMY TOMATO SOUP

*Prep* **10 MINUTES**     *Cook* **18 MINUTES**

| | |
|---|---|
| 2 | cans (14½ ounces each) diced tomatoes |
| 2 | tablespoons butter |
| 1 | medium (½ cup) onion, finely chopped |
| ¼ | cup all-purpose flour |
| ½ | teaspoon salt |
| ⅛ | teaspoon ground pepper |
| 1 | pint (2 cups) half & half |
| 1 | tablespoon sugar |
| 1 | teaspoon Worcestershire sauce |

*Here's that hot bowl of cream of tomato soup from childhood days.*

**LET'S BEGIN** Process tomatoes in a food processor until finely chopped. Sauté the onion in the butter in a large saucepot over medium-high heat for 4 minutes, or until soft.

**INTO THE PAN** Stir in the flour, salt, and pepper. Whisk in half & half. Reduce the heat to medium-low. Cook, stirring occasionally, for 4 minutes or until mixture thickens. Stir in all remaining ingredients. Cook for 5 minutes, or until heated through (do not boil).

*Makes 5 servings*

*Per serving: 240 calories, 5g protein, 21g carbohydrates, 16g fat, 10g saturated fat, 50mg cholesterol, 862mg sodium*

*Roasted Corn Chowder, page 55*

# Chowder Pot

When you're craving a rich, delicious, homemade soup, something so thick that it's almost a stew, stir up a chowder. Simmer up an old fashioned corn chowder with smoky bacon one night, with roasted chicken or tuna another. Try a typical New England fish chowder that's thickened with crackers, an American Chowder with smoky sausages and potatoes, a Midwestern pot that's brimming with corn and cheese. Learn how to adapt chowder recipes to ingredients you have on hand, and how to double the dinners from a chowder pot without a lot of extra time. Discover the smiles when you serve a chowder that bubbles up so hearty, filling, and fabulous!

# CHICKEN & RED PEPPER CORN CHOWDER

*Prep* **10 MINUTES**     *Cook* **20 MINUTES**

2   slices bacon, diced

1   small onion, chopped

¾   cup seeded and minced
    red bell pepper

1   can (10 ounces) cream
    of potato soup

1   can (14 ounces)
    creamed corn

¼   cup milk

¼   cup water

1   cup diced roasted
    chicken

*For a quick meal-in-a-bowl, make this colorful chowder. There's hardly any chopping to do, and it cooks in just minutes. Pick up some bran muffins, make a simple salad, and it's supper!*

**LET'S BEGIN**  Cook the bacon in a medium saucepan over medium heat until crispy. Drain on paper towels. Discard all but 1 tablespoon bacon fat.

**INTO THE PAN**  Sauté the onion and bell pepper in the bacon fat over medium-low heat for 6 minutes, or until the onion is soft. Stir in the potato soup, corn, milk, and water.

**HEAT & SERVE**  Increase the heat to medium and cook for 5 to 7 minutes. Add the chicken and cook for 5 minutes, or until heated through. Garnish with the crisp bacon.

*Makes 4 servings*

*Per serving: 235 calories, 15g protein, 31g carbohydrates, 7g fat, 3g saturated fat, 42mg cholesterol, 900mg sodium*

# ROASTED CORN CHOWDER

*Prep* **5 MINUTES**     *Bake/Cook* **25 MINUTES**

1     package (16 ounces) frozen whole-kernel corn

3     slices bacon, coarsely chopped

2     tablespoons butter or margarine

½     cup chopped red bell pepper

½     cup sliced celery

¼     cup sliced scallions

3     tablespoons all-purpose flour

2     cans (14 ounces each) chicken broth

1½    cups half-and-half

Chopped fresh parsley (optional)

*The secret to the fabulous flavor of this chowder is roasting the corn, which caramelizes the corn sugars. When simmered in the soup pot, the corn quickly adds a rich deep taste throughout.*

**LET'S BEGIN** Heat the oven to 425°F. Spread the corn out on a 15x10-inch jelly-roll pan. Bake for 15 to 20 minutes, tossing occasionally, until light brown and roasted. Meanwhile, sauté the bacon for 3 to 4 minutes in a large saucepan over medium heat, or until light brown. Drain.

**INTO THE PAN** Melt the butter in the same saucepan until it sizzles. Sauté the bell pepper, celery, and scallions over medium heat for 5 minutes, or until crisp-tender. Stir in the flour and cook until bubbly. Add the chicken broth and continue cooking for 3 to 5 minutes, or until it boils.

**SIMMER LOW** Reduce the heat to medium-low and stir in the roasted corn, the bacon and half-and-half. Cook, stirring, for 10 to 12 minutes. Sprinkle with parsley, if you like.

*Makes 4 servings*

*Per serving: 350 calories, 12g protein, 34g carbohydrates, 21g fat, 12g saturated fat, 54mg cholesterol, 826mg sodium*

---

## Time Savers

### DOUBLE THE CORN, DOUBLE THE DINNERS

**THE DO-AHEAD SUPPER**
When making this Roasted Corn Chowder, cook twice the amount you need, using two different pans. Refrigerate the extras.

Another night, turn the extras into one of two different chowders.

**CREOLE CHOWDER**
Substitute andouille or other spicy sausage for the bacon. During the last few minutes of cooking, drop in 12 ounces precooked, shelled, and deveined shrimp plus a generous sprinkling of hot pepper sauce.

**TEX-MEX POT**
Add a teaspoon of taco seasonings with the flour. Stir in 2 cups cooked chicken during the last 5 minutes of cooking. Top soup with crushed tortilla chips and sprinkle with chopped cilantro instead of parsley.

# COCONUT CHICKEN CHOWDER

Prep **10 MINUTES**     Cook **22 MINUTES**

*Add interest to your chowder pot with this Asian-inspired recipe.
Buy coconut milk (not the product labeled cream of coconut) and
watch the hot pepper sauce. You may need only half the amount.*

| | |
|---|---|
| 2 | tablespoons vegetable oil |
| 1 | pound boneless, skinless chicken breasts, cut into bite-size chunks |
| 1 | large celery rib, sliced |
| 1 | red bell pepper, diced |
| 1 | large scallion, thinly sliced |
| 1 | large garlic clove, minced |
| 1 | can (14 ounces) coconut milk |
| ½ | cup water |
| ¼ | cup creamy peanut butter |
| 2 | teaspoons hot pepper sauce |
| 1¼ | teaspoons salt |

**LET'S BEGIN** Heat 1 tablespoon of oil in a 3-quart saucepot over medium-high heat. Sauté the chicken for 5 minutes,
until light brown. Transfer to a plate with a slotted spoon.

**INTO THE PAN** Heat the remaining oil in the saucepot.
Add the celery and bell pepper and sauté for 5 minutes. Add
the scallion and garlic and cook 1 minute longer.

**BUBBLE & STIR** Return the chicken to the saucepot
and add the remaining ingredients. Bring to a boil over
high heat. Reduce the heat to low. Cover and simmer for
10 minutes, stirring occasionally.

*Makes 4 servings*
*Per serving: 520 calories, 33g protein, 12g carbohydrates,
40g fat, 24g saturated fat, 66mg cholesterol, 919mg sodium*

---

## Cooking Basics

### TIME-SAVING SUBSTITUTIONS

A favorite recipe's like a true and
trusted friend. It's dependable. You
can use it over and over, even if
you don't have all the ingredients
onhand. Just follow these tips for
what substitutions to make. Saves
you shopping time and money!

**MISSING MEATS**
If a chowder calls for shrimp or
fish and you don't have it, toss in
some tuna (look for the new
pouch for a fresh flavor) or some
chicken (roasted or canned) or
turkey if you have it. If not, fry up
some bacon or sliver some ham.

**THE VEGETABLE BIN**
If the recipe calls for potatoes and
you don't have any, toss in ⅓ cup
uncooked rice or ½ cup fine soup
noodles for each large potato. If a
creamy chowder asks for certain
vegetables which you don't have,
toss in carrots for celery, onions
for shallots, string beans for peas.
Tomatoes and mushrooms go
nicely into any vegetable soup.

**NO CREAM?**
If the recipe calls for cream and
you don't have it, use whole milk
or 2% milk instead. As a general
rule, in most recipes, you'll need
1 to 2 tablespoons less than the
amount of cream in recipe.

# HAM & VEGETABLE STEW

*Prep* **15 MINUTES**    *Cook* **30 MINUTES**

¼  cup butter or margarine

¼  cup all-purpose flour

¼  teaspoon each: dried basil leaves, salt, and ground black pepper

2  cups water

2  teaspoons chicken-flavored instant bouillon granules

2  cups peeled and cubed potatoes

1  cup chopped carrots

½  cup sliced scallions

2  cups half-and-half

1½  cups cubed ham

1½  cups frozen whole-kernel corn thawed

*Because of the half-and-half added at the end of the cooking time, this hearty stew's a chowder, too. It's chock full of ham and veggies. Try frozen peas or green beans instead of the corn.*

**LET'S BEGIN**  In a large saucepan over medium heat, melt the butter. Stir in the flour, basil, salt, black pepper, water, and bouillon. Cook and stir until the mixture thickens and boils.

**BUBBLE & STIR**  Add the potatoes, carrots, and scallions. Bring to a boil. Reduce the heat and simmer for 10 to 15 minutes or until the potatoes are crisp-tender.

**MIX & SERVE**  Add the half-and-half, ham, and corn, and stir until blended (do not boil). Heat thoroughly.

*Makes 6 servings*
*Per serving: 348 calories, 13g protein, 29g carbohydrates, 21g fat, 12g saturated fat, 72mg cholesterol, 1,046mg sodium*

---

## Food Facts

### HOW CHOWDER GOT ITS NAME

Chowder comes from the French word *chaudière*, the name for an iron cooking pot used by the French settlers. In the 1730s they made their home in the maritime provinces of Canada. Their neighbors were the Micmac Indians, whose diet was heavily based on local clams. The Indians placed the clams in hollowed out tree trunks, covered them with water, and added hot stones. The clams cooked—and all feasted.

Gradually, the Indian tradition of steaming the clams merged with the cooking pots of the settlers (the *chaudière*) to create what we know today as chowder. Those early chowders, which migrated to New England with the settlers, were usually made from staples, such as salt pork, sea biscuits, bread, local fish, and clams.

In the 19th century, potatoes thickened the chowders, then milk or cream was stirred in. Cooks in Rhode Island made their chowders with tomatoes and herbs, which, oddly, soon became known as Manhattan Clam Chowder.

# BLACK BEAN CHILI CHOWDER

*Prep* 5 MINUTES    *Cook* 8 MINUTES

1    can (19 ounces) black
      bean soup

1    can (14½ ounces) diced
      tomatoes with garlic and
      onion

1    can (8¾ ounces) whole
      kernel corn, drained

⅓    cup sliced scallions

¼    cup salsa

Sour cream (optional)

*Make a Tex-Mex soul happy in mere minutes with this hearty Southwestern chowder. Wrap corn or flour tortillas in foil and warm in a 350°F oven.*

**LET'S BEGIN** Combine the black bean soup, tomatoes, corn, scallions, and salsa in a large saucepan and bring to a boil. Reduce the heat to medium and cook for 3 minutes.

**SERVE IT UP** Serve with a dollop of sour cream, if you like.

*Makes 4 servings*

*Per serving: 140 calories, 6g protein, 28g carbohydrates, 2g fat, 0g saturated fat, 0mg cholesterol, 1,196mg sodium*

## Cook to Cook

### WHAT KINDS OF FISH CHOWDERS DO YOU MAKE?

❝ I like to toss both *seafood and fish together into chowders,* such as pre-cooked shrimp and cooked cod, sole, or haddock.

My family loves *scallops in chowder.* The small bay scallops are just the right size. but if you can't find them, cut the sea scallops into thirds. Add the scallops to the pot the last 3 minutes of cooking.

Our traditional soup is *fresh codfish chowder.* I cut up the fish into bite-size pieces and add them to the pot the last 2 minutes of cooking.

I like to *mix up the types of fish* in my favorite chowder recipe, but I always make sure to choose the same type of fish, whether lean or oily. Most soup recipes call for lean fish with the blander flavor and the lighter, firmer white flesh. They can

easily be substituted, pound per pound. Those fish include cod, scrod (small cod) flounder, haddock, red snapper, grouper, sea bass, and tilefish. The more delicate white fish, such as flounder and sole taste great, but they tend to fall apart as they cook in a chowder. Some chowders feature a more oily fish, with a richer flavor and darker flesh, such as bass, salmon, swordfish, trout, and tuna. ❞

# DOWN EAST FISH CHOWDER

*Prep* **30 MINUTES**      *Cook* **45 MINUTES**

*When only a traditional New England chowder will do, make this hearty fish pot. Although it calls for haddock, cod, halibut, or even snapper would all work perfectly here.*

| | |
|---|---|
| 4 | medium potatoes (about 1½ pounds) |
| 6 | ounces salt pork, diced |
| 1 | cup all-purpose flour |
| 2 | teaspoons salt |
| 1 | teaspoon ground black pepper |
| 1½ | pounds haddock fillet, cut into bite-size pieces |
| 1 | cup chopped onions |
| 2 | quarts milk (8 cups) |
| 1 | jar (4 ounces) chopped pimientos |
| 24 | crackers |
| | Chopped fresh parsley (optional) |

**LET'S BEGIN** Peel and cube the potatoes. Set aside. Sauté the pork in a large Dutch oven over medium-high heat until crisp. Transfer the pork to a plate with a slotted spoon.

**LAYER** Mix the flour, salt, and black pepper in a bowl. Layer the fish, potatoes, and onions in the pork drippings and sprinkle each layer with the flour mixture. Pour the milk over the layers and bring to a boil.

**SIMMER SLOW** Reduce the heat. Cover and simmer, stirring occasionally, for 30 minutes. Add the pork and pimientos and heat through. Break the crackers into the soup bowls and ladle in the chowder. Garnish with parsley, if you like.

*Makes 5 servings*

*Per serving: 375 calories, 20g protein, 33g carbohydrates, 18g fat, 8g saturated fat, 67mg cholesterol, 790mg sodium*

# Tuna Corn Chowdah

*Prep* **10 MINUTES**     *Cook* **10 MINUTES**

| | |
|---|---|
| 2 | tablespoons butter or margarine |
| ½ | cup each: diced carrots, celery, and onion |
| 2 | tablespoon flour |
| 1 | teaspoon dried thyme leaves |
| 1 | can (14.5 ounces) cream-style corn |
| 2 | cups milk |
| 1 | pouch (7 ounces) tuna |
| 1 | cup water |
| 1 | teaspoon chicken-flavored instant bouillon granules |

*Tuna from a convenient pouch stars in this quick corn chowder. Chop a few veggies, simmer, and serve! If you wish to substitute tuna from a can, drain it well before adding to the pot.*

**LET'S BEGIN**  In a medium saucepan, melt the butter over medium heat.  Sauté the carrots, celery, and onion for about 3 minutes, or until the vegetables are crisp-tender.

**STIR IT IN**  Add the flour and thyme to the saucepan and blend well. Cook for 1 minute. Stir in the corn, milk, tuna, water, and bouillon.

**SIMMER LOW**  Cover and simmer (do not boil) for 5 minutes to heat through, stirring occasionally.

*Makes 4 servings*

*Per serving: 302 calories, 18g protein, 31g carbohydrates, 12g fat, 7g saturated fat, 54mg cholesterol, 840mg sodium*

---

## Food Facts

### 3 GOOD REASONS TO EAT SOME TUNA

It's no secret: tuna is filled with flavor and lots of protein, too. A 3-ounce serving supplies over 45 percent of the amount of protein you need each day. It's also a great source of niacin and supplies a fair amount of those heart-healthy omega-3 fatty acids. Those are the polyunsaturated fats that do not clog the arteries in your heart.

Three ounces of white tuna packed in water has 50 fewer calories and less than half the fat, compared to the same amount packed in oil. Ounce per ounce, the tuna inside the pouch packs the same amount of goodness as that inside the can—plus a fresher taste.

And here's more good news. Tuna also contributes 53 percent of the Daily Value of niacin, which is an important nutrient for over overall heart health.

# SLIM 'N' SASSY CORN CHOWDER

*Prep* **10 MINUTES**     *Cook* **20 MINUTES**

| | |
|---|---|
| 1¼ | pounds potatoes |
| 4 | slices bacon, chopped |
| 1 | can (13¾ ounces) chicken broth |
| 1 | package (10 ounces) frozen whole-kernel corn, thawed, drained |
| ½ | cup each: chopped celery and onion |
| 2 | tablespoons flour |
| ½ | cup light salad dressing |
| 2 | cups 2% reduced fat milk |

*Speed up this fast chowder even more by microwaving the potatoes.*

**LET'S BEGIN** Peel and cube potatoes. Cook the bacon in a large saucepot until crisp; drain off fat. Stir in the potatoes, broth, corn, celery, and onion and bring to a boil. Reduce heat to low and simmer for 15 minutes, or until potatoes are tender.

**STIR IT IN** Mix the dressing and flour in a medium bowl. Stir in the milk. Add this to the potato mixture. Cook for 3 to 5 minutes, or until thoroughly heated, stirring occasionally.

*Makes 6 servings*

*Per serving: 243 calories, 8g protein, 35g carbohydrates, 8g fat, 2g saturated fat, 13mg cholesterol, 503mg sodium*

# AMERICAN CHOWDER

*Prep* **15 MINUTES**     *Cook* **25 MINUTES**

| | |
|---|---|
| 2 | tablespoons butter |
| 1 | large onion, sliced |
| 4 | cups cubed potatoes |
| 2 | cups water |
| 1 | cup sliced celery |
| 2 | teaspoons salt and ¼ teaspoon ground pepper |
| 2 | cups milk |
| 2 | tablespoons flour |
| 1 | package (12 ounces) smokie links, sliced |
| 8 | ounces pasteurized prepared cheese product |

*Here's a heart-warming chowder the whole family will love!*

**LET'S BEGIN** Melt the butter in a 3-quart saucepan over medium-high heat Sauté the onion until tender. Add the potatoes, water, celery, salt, and black pepper. Bring to a boil.

**SIMMER LOW** Reduce heat. Cover and simmer for 15 minutes. Blend a small amount of the milk into the flour, then slowly add this mixture to the hot vegetables, stirring constantly.

**BUBBLE & STIR** Stir in the remaining milk and links. Cook, stirring, for 5 minutes, or until the mixture comes to a simmer and thickens. Add the cheese and stir until melted.

*Makes 8 servings*

*Per serving: 336 calories, 12g protein, 21g carbohydrates, 23g fat, 11g saturated fat, 59mg cholesterol, 1,550mg sodium*

# POTATO CORN CHOWDER WITH CHICKEN

*Prep* **10 MINUTES**     *Cook* **20 MINUTES**

| | |
|---|---|
| 1 | tablespoon oil |
| 1 | cup uncooked chicken cubes (about 1 chicken breast) |
| ½ | cup chopped onion |
| 1 | cup water |
| 1 | medium potato, peeled and cut in ½-inch cubes |
| 1 | package original country gravy mix |
| 2 | cups milk |
| 1 | cup whole kernel corn |
| 1 | bay leaf |

*For the fastest chowder around, make this one-pot wonder. Double the recipe and make enough for four, if you like. Sprinkle it with oyster crackers, make an iceberg lettuce salad, and enjoy!*

**LET'S BEGIN** Heat the oil over medium-high heat in a large saucepan. Add the chicken and onion and sauté for 3 minutes. Stir in the water and potatoes and bring to a boil. Reduce the heat, cover, and simmer for 5 minutes, or until potatoes are tender.

**STIR IT IN** Blend the gravy mix and milk together. Add the gravy mixture and remaining ingredients to the saucepan. Bring to a boil.

**SIMMER SLOW** Reduce the heat, cover and simmer, stirring occasionally, for 10 minutes, or until the flavors blend. Remove the bay leaf before serving.

*Makes 5 servings*

*Per serving: 235 calories, 11g protein, 30g carbohydrates, 8g fat, 3g saturated fat, 28mg cholesterol, 550mg sodium*

# PEPPY BAKED POTATO SOUP

*Prep* **10 MINUTES**       *Cook* **30 MINUTES**

1    cup sliced pepperoni, cut into ¼-inch-wide strips

1    tablespoon butter or oil

1    medium onion, chopped

1    garlic clove, minced

2    medium baking potatoes, peeled and cut into bite-size pieces

1    can (14½ ounces) chicken broth

½    cup heavy cream

**Sour cream, shredded Cheddar cheese, and snipped fresh chives (optional)**

*Here's a fast way to cut presliced pepperoni into strips: stack the slices in small piles and then cut into strips with a sharp knife.*

**LET'S BEGIN**  Cook the pepperoni in a medium skillet over medium heat for 4 minutes, or until crisp. Transfer the pepperoni to paper towels to drain, then set aside. Discard the drippings.

**BUBBLE & STIR**  Melt butter in a medium saucepan over medium heat. Sauté onion for 3 minutes and stir in garlic. Add potatoes and broth and bring to a boil. Reduce the heat. Cover and simmer for 20 minutes, or until potatoes are tender.

**SERVE IT UP**  Stir in the cream. Ladle the soup into bowls and sprinkle with the pepperoni. Garnish with sour cream, Cheddar, and chives, if you like.

*Makes 4 servings*

*Per serving: 460 calories, 15g protein, 23g carbohydrates, 35g fat, 18g saturated fat, 92mg cholesterol, 1,047mg sodium*

# LEEK & POTATO POT

*Prep* **15 MINUTES**   *Cook* **30 MINUTES**

*If you haven't yet discovered the magic of leeks in potato soup, now's your chance. They contribute both onion and garlic flavors as they simmer. The best part: soup's "on" in half an hour!*

¼ cup butter or margarine

2 large leeks, chopped

4 all-purpose potatoes, peeled and diced

4 cups chicken broth or stock

1 tablespoon green pepper sauce

¼ teaspoon salt

Sour cream or yogurt

Snipped fresh chives

**LET'S BEGIN** Melt the butter in a large soup pot over medium heat. Add the leeks and sauté for 5 minutes, or until crisp-tender.

**INTO THE PAN** Add the potatoes to the pot and cook 5 minutes longer. Stir in the broth, pepper sauce, and salt. Bring to a boil over high heat. Reduce the heat to low. Cover and simmer 15 minutes, or until the potatoes are tender.

**PROCESS IT SMOOTH** Purée the soup, in batches if necessary, in a food processor or blender. Ladle into serving bowls and top with a dollop of sour cream and sprinkle with chives.

*Makes 6 servings*

*Per serving: 200 calories, 5g protein, 24g carbohydrates, 9g fat, 5g saturated fat, 22mg cholesterol, 709mg sodium*

*On the Menu*

Here's a fast-to-fix menu with a French touch. It's perfect for an instant party!

*Leek & Potato Pot*

*Warm Baguettes Stuffed with Thin Ham Slices*

*Bibb Lettuce with Herb-Wine Vinaigrette*

*Strawberry Tart*

*French-Roast Coffee Mineral Water*

*Italian Pepperoni Minestrone, page 82*

# Soups on Tour

Pick up your soup pot, grab a ladle, and enjoy a tasting holiday with one of our "touring" soups. They're based on authentic recipes from folks here and far—all Americanized to fit into our fast-paced lives. Quickly simmer up some chicken chili like they do in the Southwest or a gumbo as in the bayou country. Try a Greek version of chicken soup with orzo. Or, if you prefer Italian, stir up a pot of Zuppa di Pesce, chock full of the fresh catch of the day, or a hearty rice and bean from the rolling hills of Tuscany. Discover many tasty, terrific, and tempting ways to serve soups and stews—all made faster than their authentic cousins.

*SuperQuick*

# SANTA FE CHICKEN SOUP

*Prep* **10 MINUTES**    *Cook* **14 MINUTES**

1    can (49 ounces) chicken broth

1    package (10 ounces) Southwestern sliced cooked chicken breast

1    can (15 ounces) pintos beans, rinsed and drained

1    can (11 ounces) Mexican-style corn, undrained

1    can (10 ounces) diced tomatoes with mild green chilies, undrained

½    cup quick-cooking rice

2 to 3 tablespoons chopped fresh cilantro

1    lime, thinly sliced

Flour tortillas, warmed (optional)

*Come to Santa Fe, where they like their chicken soup with a Mexican flair. You'll often find green chilies in the pot, along with pinto beans, and cilantro, too.*

**LET'S BEGIN** Combine the first five ingredients in a large soup pot. Bring to a boil over medium-high heat and stir in the rice.

**SIMMER LOW** Reduce the heat to low. Cover and simmer for 10 minutes, or until the rice is tender. Remove from the heat and stir in the cilantro.

**SERVE** Ladle the soup into bowls and garnish each serving with a slice of lime. Serve with a basket of warm flour tortillas, if desired.

*Makes 6 servings*

*Per serving: 256 calories, 25g protein, 31g carbohydrates, 3g fat, 1g saturated fat, 40mg cholesterol, 1,332mg sodium*

# SOUP PARMESANO
*Prep* **10 MINUTES**      *Cook* **20 MINUTES**

1    **pound ground chicken**

1    **package (¾ ounce) dried Italian salad dressing mix**

1    **tablespoon olive oil**

6    **cans (10½ ounces each) chicken broth (or 2 quarts)**

½    **cup frozen carrot slices**

1    **package (9 ounces) refrigerated pasta, such as cheese-filled tortellini**

1    **can (14½ ounces) diced tomatoes, drained**

½    **cup chopped fresh spinach or thawed, chopped frozen spinach**

*Here's a quick supper soup with the flavors from Italy that's fast to fix and hearty enough to please even the hungriest folks. Double the meatballs and freeze half for a second pot of soup another day.*

**LET'S BEGIN**  Mix together ground turkey and salad dressing mix in a medium bowl. Form into 1-inch balls. Heat oil in skillet; add meatballs and brown on medium heat for 7 to 10 minutes. Drain meatballs on paper towels.

**BUBBLE & BOIL**  Meanwhile, bring broth to a boil in a large stockpot. Add tortellini and carrots. Cook for 5 minutes.

**SIMMER LOW**  Reduce the heat and add the meatballs, then simmer gently for 10 minutes. Add the tomatoes and spinach and stir just until the spinach wilts slightly.

*Makes 4 servings*

*Per serving: 560 calories, 40g protein, 38g carbohydrates, 26g fat, 3g saturated fat, 34mg cholesterol, 2,895mg sodium*

# GREEK AVGOLEMONO SOUP WITH CHICKEN

*Prep* **10 MINUTES**     *Cook* **20 MINUTES**

*The literal translation of the Greek avgolemono is "egg-lemon," which is exactly what this soup contains. Toss in some orzo and chicken and you'll think you're on the Greek isles.*

| | |
|---|---|
| 4 | cups chicken broth |
| 1 | cup water |
| ½ | cup orzo |
| 2 | teaspoons dried Greek seasoning |
| 3 | large egg yolks |
| 1 | tablespoon cornstarch |
| 1 | cup shredded cooked chicken or turkey |
| 2 | tablespoons fresh lemon juice |
| 4 | thin lemon slices (optional) |

Chopped fresh parsley (optional)

**LET'S BEGIN** Combine the broth, ¾ cup of the water, the orzo, and Greek seasoning in a medium saucepan and bring to a boil. Reduce the heat. Cover and simmer, covered, for 9 to 10 minutes, or until the orzo is just tender.

**STIR IT IN** Whisk the egg yolks, the remaining ¼ cup water, and the cornstarch in a large bowl. Gradually whisk in about 2 cups of the hot broth mixture, then whisk back into the saucepan. Cook over medium-low heat for 5 to 7 minutes, until slightly thickened. (Do not let it boil.) Stir in the chicken and lemon juice and heat through.

**SERVE** Ladle the soup into bowls and garnish each serving with a thin slice of lemon and chopped parsley, if you wish.

*Makes 4 servings*

*Per serving: 217 calories, 18g protein, 20g carbohydrates, 7g fat, 2g saturated fat, 191mg cholesterol, 625mg sodium*

---

## On the Menu

*Take a tour to the blue Aegean where the dining is leisurely and luscious.*

*Stuffed Grape Leaves*

*Greek Avgolemono Soup with Chicken*

*Warmed Pita with Hummus*

*Greek Salad with Feta*

*Baklava*

*Tea with Fresh Mint*

# TORTILLA CHICKEN CHILI

*Prep* **10 MINUTES**     *Cook* **19 MINUTES**

1   tablespoon vegetable oil

1   pound boneless, skinless chicken breasts, cut into ¾-inch chunks

1   package (1¼ ounces) chili seasoning

1   can (14½ ounces) diced tomatoes, undrained

1   can (15 to 16 ounces) white kidney or pinto beans, undrained

1   can (11 ounces) plain or Mexican-style whole kernel corn, drained

½   cup water

1½  cups broken tortilla chips (bite-size pieces)

Shredded Cheddar cheese

Sour cream

Chopped fresh cilantro

*In Mexico, the tortilla is the everyday bread—round, flat, thin, unleavened. In this chili, fried tortilla chips add authenticity.*

**LET'S BEGIN** Heat the oil in a large nonstick skillet over medium-high heat. Cook the chicken, stirring, for 5 minutes, or until light brown.

**SIMMER IT SLOW** Stir in the chili seasoning, tomatoes and their juices, beans, corn, water, and tortilla chips. Bring to a boil. Reduce the heat. Cover and simmer, stirring occasionally for 10 minutes to allow the flavors to blend.

**SERVE** Ladle the soup into bowls and top with Cheddar, sour cream, and cilantro.

*Makes 6 servings*
*Per serving: 260 calories, 24g protein, 29g carbohydrates, 6g fat, 1g saturated fat, 44mg cholesterol, 1,125mg sodium*

## Cooking Basics

### 5 SIMPLE STEPS TO PERFECT SOUP

**1. Start with the right pot,** preferably a large, deep soup pot with a lid.

**2. Begin with a sauté,** by quickly cooking a few vegetables in a little oil over high heat. This gives an aromatic foundation to your pot of soup. The French call it a *mirepoix*; the Italians, a *soffritto*; other cooks, their "little secret."

**3. Add tomatoes last to the sauté,** as their juices will prevent the other ingredients from browning nicely.

**4. Now add the cooking liquid,** the rest of the ingredients and the fresh or dried herbs and spices—but just a little salt. Since the flavors intensify as the soup simmers, salt the soup sparingly at the beginning.

**5. Simmer low!** Soups are a great fix-and-forget dish. Just put all the ingredients together and let it simmer away. Most recipes call for covering the pot. But never never boil the pot. Simmer it over a low heat instead!

## HOW CAN I CHANGE MY FAVORITE SOUP RECIPES INTO STEWS?

❝ When a recipe calls for ground beef, I substitute *cubes of beef sirloin.* This quickly turns the soup into a heartier, more filling stew. If a recipe calls for potatoes, increase them. If not, add them.

In the beginning, be sure to *dredge the cubes of meat in seasoned flour* then sauté them until they're nice and brown. The flour helps to thicken and season the stew as it simmers.

I always do what the Italians do: add some *small pieces of country bread* and let them dissolve and thicken the soup as it cooks. It turns into a peasant country-style stew.

Or follow what cooks in Mexico have done for centuries: *add strips of tortillas to the stew pot.* As the stew cooks, the tortillas soak up some of the liquid and the dish becomes a stew.

To thicken a soup fast: *add some quick-cooking rice.* As it cooks, rice soaks up extra liquid, turning a soup into a stew. ❞

*SuperQuick*
# MEXICAN TACO STEW

*Prep* **10 MINUTES**     *Cook* **10 MINUTES**

*Here are all the fixings of a Tex-Mex taco, thrown into the stew pot. Beef, salsa, cheese, crisp tortilla chips—they're all called for. Simmer them up for a few minutes and supper's ready.*

1     **pound lean ground beef**

2     **jars (16 ounces each) thick-and-chunky salsa**

2     **cans (14½ ounces each) beef broth**

1     **can (7 ounces) whole-kernel corn, undrained**

**Tortilla chips, crushed**

**Mexican blend shredded cheese**

**LET'S BEGIN** Cook the beef in a large sauce pot over medium heat until no longer pink, breaking it up with the side of a spoon. Drain off the fat.

**STIR IT IN** Add the salsa, broth, and corn to the pot and bring to a boil. Reduce the heat and simmer for 5 minutes, or until heated through.

**SERVE** Ladle the stew into bowls and top with the tortilla chips and cheese.

*Makes 9 servings*

*Per serving: 193 calories, 14g protein, 14g carbohydrates, 9g fat, 4g saturated fat, 35mg cholesterol, 1,151mg sodium*

# COCONUT SHRIMP STEW

*Prep* **5 MINUTES**     *Cook* **15 MINUTES**

1   cup chicken broth

2   tablespoons Tex-Mex chili beef seasonings

2   teaspoons sugar

½   teaspoon ground cinnamon

½   pound sweet potatoes, peeled and cut into ½-inch chunks

1   can (14 ounces) unsweetened coconut milk

1   pound large shrimp, peeled and deveined

1   large ripe plantain or 2 bananas, peeled and sliced

*Visit Latin America and expect stews like this one with shrimp, coconut milk, and a "cooking banana" called a plantain. Here, it's in a stew that's spiced with sweet cinnamon and hot chili seasonings.*

**LET'S BEGIN** Bring the first 4 ingredients to a boil in a large saucepot over high heat.

**STIR IT IN** Add the sweet potatoes. Cover and boil for 5 minutes, or until the potatoes are almost tender.

**SIMMER LOW** Reduce the heat to medium-low and add the remaining ingredients. Simmer, stirring occasionally, for 5 minutes, or just until the shrimp turn pink.

*Makes 5 servings*

*Per serving: 402 calories, 23g protein, 34g carbohydrates, 21g fat, 17g saturated fat, 138mg cholesterol, 537mg sodium*

---

## Food Facts

### 3 EASY WAYS TO SAVE CENTS IN THE STEW POT

**#1 GO ETHNIC!**
Head for the Spanish, Italian, or Asian markets to shop for spices and other products commonly used in that country's cuisine. The selection is better—and so are the prices.

**#2 CHEESE-WISE**
When you're buying cheeses to melt into a soup, buy the less expensive store brands (choose the extra, sharp Cheddars). But if cheese is a special element in the dish, you'll save money in the long run if you buy a small amount of a top-quality, strong-flavored cheese because you won't need quite as much to make a delicious dish. For example, when sprinkling on top of the soup, splurge on those fancy imported Parmesans or English Cheddars. And for melting on top of croutons for onion soup, buy real Gruyère.

**#3 TRANSFORM LEFTOVERS**
Use bones from the roasted chicken in your stews: the meat attached will cook off the bones into the soup and bones add a flavor-boost, too. Just remove before serving.

# SPICY SENEGALESE SOUP

*Prep* **10 MINUTES**    *Cook* **33 MINUTES**

1    tablespoon unsalted butter

1    large onion, chopped

4    garlic cloves, chopped

2    tablespoons all-purpose flour

4    teaspoons curry powder

2    cans (14½ ounces each) chicken broth

½    cup water

1    tart cooking apple, peeled, cored, and sliced

1    cup thinly sliced carrots

¼    cup golden raisins

¼    cup cayenne pepper sauce

1    cup half-and-half

*Travel to Africa where many cooks grind their own curry powder to make that incredibly deep spicy flavor. But you can use any curry powder for this recipe. Generally, curry contains such spices as ground kari leaves, cumin, coriander, mustard, black and red peppers, fenugreek, and turmeric.*

**LET'S BEGIN** Melt the butter in a large saucepan over medium heat. Sauté the onion and garlic for 5 minutes, or until softened. Whisk in the flour and curry powder. Cook, whisking, for 1 minute.

**SIMMER LOW** Gradually stir in the broth and water. Add the apple, carrots, raisins, and pepper sauce and bring to a boil. Reduce the heat. Cover and simmer for 25 minutes, or until the carrots are tender.

**PURÉE IT SMOOTH** Purée the soup in batches in a food processor or blender. Return the soup to the saucepan and stir in the half-and-half. Cook on low heat for 2 minutes, or until heated through.

*Makes 4 servings*

*Per serving: 250 calories, 8g protein, 29g carbohydrates, 12g fat, 7g saturated fat, 30mg cholesterol, 790mg sodium*

## Microwave in Minutes

### MICROWAVE THIS SOUP IN HALF THE TIME

Cook this Senegalese Soup in the microwave in 50 percent less time: Melt the butter in a covered 2-quart microwavable dish on High, stir in the onion and garlic and microwave for 2 minutes. Whisk in the flour and curry powder and cook 1 minute longer. Whisk in 1½ cups of broth and add the apples and carrots. Cover and microwave on high for 8 to 10 minutes, or until the carrots are tender. Stir in the remaining ingredients and microwave 3 to 5 minutes longer. Purée.

# ZUPPA DI PESCE

*Prep* **5 MINUTES**      *Cook* **25 MINUTES**

*In Italian, zuppa is the word for soup; pesce, for fish. In Italy, this soup varies from village to village, depending upon the day's local catch. Toss in some littleneck clams or mussels, too, if you like.*

| | |
|---|---|
| ¼ | cup olive oil |
| 1 | medium onion, chopped |
| 2 | garlic cloves, minced |
| 1 | can (28 ounces) whole plum tomatoes, undrained |
| ½ | cup dry white wine or water |
| 2 | tablespoons thinly sliced fresh basil |
| 2 | pounds fish fillets, such as cod, red snapper, orange roughy or a mixture, cut into chunks |

**Grated Parmesan cheese**

**LET'S BEGIN**  Heat the oil in a large saucepan over medium heat. Sauté the onion and garlic for 4 to 5 minutes, until softened.

**SIMMER LOW**  Stir in the tomatoes with their liquid, wine, and basil and bring to a boil. Reduce the heat and simmer for 10 minutes.

**COOK & SERVE**  Add the fish and simmer 10 minutes longer, or until the fish is opaque throughout. Sprinkle with the cheese.

*Makes 4 servings*

*Per serving: 391 calories, 43g protein, 12g carbohydrates, 15g fat, 2g saturated fat, 98mg cholesterol, 550mg sodium*

---

## Cooking Basics

### 5 AMAZING SOUP RESCUES

**SOUP TOO SALTY?**
Drop in a few thin slices of peeled potatoes. Simmer for 15 minutes. When the potato slices turn translucent, they have soaked up their "quota" of salt. Discard.

**SOUP TOO THIN?**
Purée some of the cooked solid ingredients from the soup in a food processor and return to the pot.

Add small bread cubes to the soup and cook until they break up.

To thicken a tomato soup, whisk in some canned tomato paste until blended.

**HAS SOUP CURDLED?**
If a cream soup curdles, strain it through a sieve, or purée it in a food processor or blender.

**BROTH TOO CLOUDY?**
Stir in 2 egg whites for each 6 cups of hot soup. They will attract the cloudy particles and float them to the top. Then just skim them off!

**SOUP TASTE WATERY?**
Add depth of flavor to your soup pot. Drizzle some red wine into tomato- and meat-based soups. Add some white wine or fresh lemon juice to chicken, fish, or vegetable-based soups.

# CHICKEN & RICE GUMBO

*Prep* **10 MINUTES**    *Cook* **24 MINUTES**

| | |
|---|---|
| 1 | pound boneless, skinless chicken breasts |
| 1 | can (14½ ounces) no salt added stewed tomatoes |
| 3 | cans (14½ ounces each) reduced-sodium chicken broth |
| 1 | can (15 ounces) whole-kernel corn, drained |
| ½ | teaspoon hot pepper sauce |
| ½ | cup quick-cooking rice |

*In New Orleans, gumbo usually comes as a stew, thickened with okra or filé powder. This one's thickened with rice.*

**LET'S BEGIN** Cut chicken into bite-size pieces and put into pot. Chop the tomatoes and add to pot with their juices. Add all remaining ingredients except rice. Bring to a boil.

**SIMMER LOW** Reduce the heat. Cover and simmer for 15 minutes. Stir in the rice and simmer for 5 minutes, or until chicken is cooked through. Serve with crackers if you like.

> *Makes 10 servings*
> *Per serving: 138 calories, 14g protein, 18g carbohydrates, 1g fat, 0g saturated fat, 26mg cholesterol, 418mg sodium*

---

*SuperQuick*

# SPANISH SEAFOOD STEW

*Prep* **10 MINUTES**    *Cook* **15 MINUTES**

| | |
|---|---|
| 2½ | pounds cod, haddock, or snapper fillets |
| 24 | little neck clams or mussels |
| 1 | jar (16 ounces) each: chunky salsa with cilantro and chunky roasted pepper and garlic salsa |
| 1 | bottle (8 ounces) clam juice |
| ¼ | cup white wine or water |
| 1 | package (3½ ounces) chorizo, sliced |
| 3 | cups hot cooked rice |

*Along the seacoast in Spain, seafood stew is always on the menu. Which fish or seafood goes into the pot depends on the day's catch.*

**LETS BEGIN** Cut the fish into large chunks. Scrub the clams or mussels and debeard the mussels, if using, with a paring knife. Combine the salsas, clam juice, and wine in a large saucepot. Add the chorizo, fish, and clams.

**SIMMER LOW** Bring to a boil. Reduce the heat. Cover and simmer for 10 minutes or until the clams and mussels open and the fish is opaque in the center.

**SERVE** Divide rice among soup bowls and ladle soup over.

> *Makes 8 servings*
> *Per serving: 338 calories, 40g protein, 25g carbohydrates, 7g fat, 2g saturated fat, 91mg cholesterol, 1,134mg sodium*

On the Menu

*Take a trip to Tuscany, where foods are hearty and fresh— just like this soup meal.*

*Tuscan Rice & Bean Soup*

*Fresh Spinach Salad with Red Wine Vinaigrette*

*Fontina Cheese*

*Warm Country Bread*

*Fresh Melon with Assorted Berries*

*SuperQuick*

# TUSCAN RICE & BEAN SOUP

Prep **5 MINUTES**     Cook **21 MINUTES**

*In the hills of Tuscany, soups are homey, filling, and brimming with flavor. Bring those same flavors to this soup with highly seasoned Italian sausages and some freshly grated Parmesan.*

| | |
|---|---|
| 8 | ounces sweet Italian sausage links, casings removed |
| 1 | can (28 ounces) diced tomatoes |
| 3 | cans 16 ounces) low-sodium chicken broth |
| ½ | teaspoon salt |
| ¼ | teaspoon cracked black peppercorns |
| ¼ | teaspoon dried oregano, crumbled |
| 1 | cup uncooked long-grain white rice |
| 1 | can (15½ ounces) Great Northern beans, undrained |

**Freshly grated Parmesan cheese (optional)**

**LET'S BEGIN**  Cook the sausage in a medium saucepan over medium-high heat for 6 minutes, or until browned, breaking it up with the side of a spoon. Drain off the fat.

**STIR IT IN**  Stir in the tomatoes, broth, salt, pepper, and oregano.

**SIMMER LOW**  Bring to a boil, then stir in the rice and beans. Cover and simmer for 15 to 20 minutes, until rice is tender. Sprinkle with fresh Parmesan cheese if you wish.

*Makes 6 servings*

*Per serving: 358 calories, 19g protein, 46g carbohydrates, 10g fat, 4g saturated fat, 29mg cholesterol, 1,331mg sodium*

# ITALIAN PEPPERONI MINESTRONE

*Prep* **20 MINUTES**     *Cook* **45 MINUTES**

| | |
|---|---|
| 7 | cups beef broth or water |
| 2 | cups coarsely chopped green cabbage |
| 1 | can (14½ ounces) Italian-style stewed tomatoes |
| 1 | medium onion, sliced |
| 1 | medium carrot, sliced |
| 1 | tablespoon Italian seasoning |
| 1 | package (9 ounces) frozen Italian green beans |
| 1 | large zucchini, halved lengthwise and sliced crosswise |
| ½ | cup bow-tie pasta or elbow macaroni |
| 1 | package (3½ ounces) pepperoni slices, quartered |
| 1 | can (15 to 16 ounces) chickpeas or red kidney beans, rinsed and drained |

**Garlic salt and ground black pepper**

**Grated Parmesan cheese**

**Saltine crackers**

Minestra (*the Italian word for soup*) *usually refers to a soup that's medium-thick. Minestrone* (*big soup*) *describes a thick vegetable soup with beans and pasta. Frozen and canned veggies speed it up.*

**LET'S BEGIN** Combine the first six ingredients in a Dutch oven or large saucepot and bring to a boil. Reduce the heat and simmer, partially covered, for 20 minutes.

**STIR IT IN** Add the green beans, zucchini, and pasta. Simmer, uncovered, stirring occasionally, for 15 minutes, or until the vegetables and pasta are tender. Stir in the pepperoni and beans and heat through. Season to taste with garlic salt and pepper.

**SERVE** Ladle the soup into bowls, sprinkle with the Parmesan, and serve with crackers alongside.

*Makes 6 to 8 servings*

*Per serving: 282 calories, 14g protein, 37g carbohydrates, 9g fat, 3g saturated fat, 13mg cholesterol, 1,623mg sodium*

---

## Cooking Basics

### FIX SOUP FIXINGS FASTER!

**SKIP THE CHOPPING**

Minutes can be saved when making a pot of soup—just by skipping the chopping. Buy pre-chopped garlic in oil and sliced-up ingredients from the salad bar. Or use frozen corn, peas, or small white onions. Just add them straight out of the freezer and toss into the hot soup during the last few minutes of cooking.

**PULSE AWAY!**

Choose the food processor blades carefully. The thicker slicing blades are good for slicing up potatoes and the chopping blade is best for chopping hard vegetables, such as carrots, bell peppers, and onions. Chop the crisper ones first like carrots, then the softer ones. To chop, not purée, pulse the processor as you go.

# COLD SPANISH VEGETABLE SOUP

*Prep* **15 MINUTES**    *Chill* **24 HOURS**

¾  cup fresh bread crumbs

3  tablespoons red wine vinegar

1  clove garlic, crushed with the side of a large knife

¼  cup olive oil

1  large cucumber, peeled and chopped

1  green bell pepper, chopped

8  large tomatoes, peeled and chopped

1  cup cold water

½  teaspoon salt

⅛  teaspoon ground black pepper

Chopped natural (unblanched) almonds

*In the Andalusia region in southern Spain, gazpachos are a country tradition, especially in the summertime. Authentically, they're thickened with fresh bread crumbs, as here.*

**LET'S BEGIN** Mix the first 4 ingredients vigorously with a fork in a small bowl to form a smooth paste. Set aside. Mix together all of the remaining ingredients in a large bowl. Stir in the bread paste until well blended.

**LET IT CHILL** Cover the bowl and refrigerate for at least 24 hours before serving. Garnish with chopped almonds.

### Makes 4 servings

*Per serving: 287 calories, 6g protein, 34g carbohydrates, 16g fat, 2g saturated fat, 0mg cholesterol, 497mg sodium*

---

## Time Savers

### TAKE SHORTCUTS IN THE SOUP POT

Here, a few ways to cut both the preparation and cooking times for the soup pot. Freeze your homemade stocks in quart-size plastic self-sealing freezer bags. **Substitute frozen vegetables for fresh**—and save preparation time. They don't require cleaning, no extra chopping (buy the chopped variety), and cook quicker than fresh.

**Keep fast soup-makings on-hand.** Stock the pantry with quick-cooking 5-minute rice, canned diced tomatoes (look for those with garlic, onion, and spices), and cans of broth. Stock the freezer with fresh pasta, strips of skinless chicken breasts, and chopped onion, garlic, celery, and carrots. Freeze some bags of your homemade pasta sauce, too.

# SPANISH ALMOND SOUP

*Prep* **15 MINUTES**     *Cook* **40 MINUTES**

2    tablespoons olive oil

4    large onions, sliced
     (about 4 cups)

½    cup blanched whole
     almonds, toasted

2    cans (14½ ounces each)
     reduced-sodium chicken
     broth

¾    cup dry white wine or
     water

1    bay leaf

1    teaspoon ground cumin

Salt and ground black pepper

4    slices French bread,
     toasted

¼    cup grated Parmesan
     cheese

2    tablespoons sliced
     almonds, toasted

*The Spanish often use nuts, like toasted almonds, to thicken their soups. Here, they're one of the main ingredients, along with onions. Make it early in the day if you wish and heat right before serving.*

**LET'S BEGIN**   Heat the oil in a medium saucepan over medium heat. Sauté the onions for 10 minutes, or until transparent. Meanwhile, very finely grind the whole almonds in a blender or food processor. Pour in 1 cup of the broth and blend until very smooth. Add the almond mixture to the onions along with the remaining broth, wine, and bay leaf.

**SIMMER IT SLOW**   Bring to a simmer. Cover and cook for 20 minutes. Stir in the cumin and simmer for 10 minutes longer. Season the soup to taste with salt and pepper.

**BROIL &S SERVE**   Preheat the broiler. Ladle the soup into ovenproof bowls. Top each with a slice of toast and sprinkle with 1 tablespoon of the cheese. Place in the broiler pan. Broil about 5 inches from the heat, watching closely, for 20 to 30 seconds, just until light brown. Sprinkle with the sliced almonds.

*Makes 4 servings*
*Per serving: 405 calories, 14g protein, 36g carbohydrates, 21g fat, 3g saturated fat, 4mg cholesterol, 807mg sodium*

*SuperQuick*

# GREEK PILAF

*Prep* **15 MINUTES**     *Cook* **6 MINUTES**

| | |
|---|---|
| 3 | ounces uncooked dried rosamarina or orzo pasta |
| 1 | tablespoon butter |
| ½ | cup chopped green or yellow bell pepper |
| 2 | large garlic cloves, minced |
| ¼ | cup chopped onion |
| 1 | cup garbanzo beans, rinsed and drained |
| 1 | can (14½ ounces) diced tomatoes with basil, garlic, and oregano, undrained |
| 1 | jar (6 ounces) marinated artichoke hearts, drained and cut up |
| ¼ | teaspoon salt |

*In the Near East, pilafs start by browning the rice in butter or oil before cooking it in stock. This variation uses pasta: either rosamarina (pumpkin-seed shape) or orzo (rice-shaped) instead of rice.*

**LET'S BEGIN** Cook pasta according to package directions. Drain and keep warm.

**INTO THE PAN** Meanwhile, melt the butter in a large saucepot over medium-high heat until sizzling. Add the bell pepper, onion, and garlic. Cook, stirring occasionally, for 3 minutes, or until al dente.

**MIX & SERVE** Stir in the cooked pasta and all of the remaining ingredients. Cook 3 minutes more, or until heated through.

*Makes 2 servings*

*Per serving: 558 calories, 16g protein, 78g carbohydrates, 22g fat, 7g saturated fat, 16g cholesterol, 2,000mg sodium*

# WARMING ASIAN CHICKEN SOUP

*Prep* **5 MINUTES**     *Cook* **25 MINUTES**

4    boneless, skinless chicken breast halves (about 1¼ pounds), cut into thin strips

8    cups chicken broth

1    tablespoon chili paste

1    piece (4 inches) unpeeled fresh ginger, coarsely chopped

2    tablespoons dark sesame oil

4    boneless, skinless chicken breast halves (about 1¼ pounds), cut into thin strips

2    carrots, diced

1    cup snow peas, trimmed and thinly sliced

4    scallions, sliced

1    cup fresh bean sprouts

½    cup loosely packed fresh mint leaves, chopped

*Quick-cooking clear soups with crisp vegetables floating in them are popular in Asian countries. Even the fast-cooking vegetables are typical of that region, such as bean sprouts and snow peas.*

**LET'S BEGIN**  Combine the broth, chili paste, ginger, and sesame oil in a Dutch oven or soup pot and bring to a boil over high heat. Reduce the heat and simmer for 15 minutes.

**MIX IT UP**  Meanwhile, put the chicken and carrots into another large pot. Strain the broth mixture over the chicken.

**SIMMER LOW**  Simmer for 3 minutes. Stir in the snow peas and cook for 1 minute. Stir in the scallions, bean sprouts, and mint and simmer for 2 minutes.

*Makes 4 servings*
*Per serving: 329 calories, 44g protein, 9g carbohydrates, 12g fat, 2g saturated fat, 82mg cholesterol, 1,696mg sodium*

*Hoppin' John Soup, page 108*

# Meal in a Pot

Here's the easiest, fastest way to simmer up supper—all in one pot! And what good eating you're in store for. Simmer up a hearty pot of Soul City Chili, a spicy pot of Shrimp Creole, a lucky pot of Hoppin' John Soup. Discover how fast you can toss ingredients into the stew pot, sauce pot, or slow-cooker—then turn the heat down to low and forget it until dinner time. There is a taco soup to simmer, beef stews to savor, and a sausage stew to enjoy. You'll find a way to cook a bean soup in half the time and how to turn your favorite kettle of soup into a meal. Pick a pot, choose a recipe, and discover how simple it is to deliver dinner in one convenient dish.

# HEARTY BLACK BEAN BOWL

*Prep* **10 MINUTES**    *Cook* **40 MINUTES**

1   package (1 pound) bacon, cut into 1-inch pieces

2   celery ribs, sliced (1 cup)

1   large onion, chopped (1 cup)

2   garlic cloves, minced

2   cans (15 ounces each) black beans, drained and rinsed

1   jar (16 ounces) picante sauce

1½   cups water

2   teaspoons instant chicken-flavored bouillon granules

1   teaspoon crushed red pepper flakes

1   tablespoon chopped fresh cilantro

Sour cream (optional)

Cornbread

*Here's a superfast way to cut up the bacon. Remove it from the package—don't separate the slices. Then, with a long, thin knife, cut the bacon crosswise into 1-inch-wide pieces. You're done!*

**LET'S BEGIN** Cook the bacon, celery, onion, and garlic in a large saucepan over medium heat, stirring occasionally, for 7 minutes, or until the bacon is crisp. Drain off the fat.

**EASY COOK** Stir in all the remaining ingredients except the cilantro. Bring to a boil over high heat. Reduce the heat. Cover and simmer, stirring occasionally, for 30 minutes.

**SERVE** Stir in the cilantro. Spoon into soup bowls, top with sour cream, and serve with corn bread, if you like.

### Makes 6 servings

*Per serving: 534 calories, 30g protein, 29g carbohydrates, 33g fat, 11g saturated fat, 81mg cholesterol, 2,962mg sodium*

---

### Microwave in Minutes

#### COOK BEAN SOUP IN HALF THE TIME

Use your microwave to help you speed-cook this bean soup in half the time.

Cook the bacon, celery, onion, and garlic in a covered, microwavable, 3-quart glass casserole on High for 8 to 10 minutes, stirring occasionally. Drain off the fat. Add all of the remaining ingredients except the cilantro. Cover and microwave on High for 15 minutes. Let the soup stand, still covered, for 5 minutes. Stir in the cilantro.

# TUSCAN CHICKEN & WHITE BEAN POT

*Prep* **15 MINUTES**    *Cook* **30 MINUTES**

| | |
|---|---|
| 6 | chicken thighs (about 1½ pounds) boned |
| 1 | bunch flat-leaf parsley |
| 3 | cups water |
| 3 | tablespoons naturally brewed soy sauce |
| 1 | large onion, chopped (1 cup) |
| ½ | cup diced carrot |
| ½ | cup diced celery |
| ½ | teaspoon dried marjoram, crumbled |
| 1 | can (15 ounces) cannellini, navy, or Great Northern beans, drained |
| 1 | tablespoon vinegar |

*To put this soup together even faster, chop the onion and dice the carrot and celery in a food processor in an instant instead.*

**LET'S BEGIN** Put the chicken and half of the parsley into a Dutch oven or soup pot. Pour in the water and soy sauce.

**SIMMER LOW** Cover the pot and bring to a boil. Reduce the heat and simmer for 10 minutes. Using a slotted spoon, transfer the chicken to a plate and discard the parsley. Add the onion, carrot, celery, and marjoram to the pot. Cover and simmer for 15 minutes.

**GET IT READY** Meanwhile, remove and discard the skin from the chicken. Cut the chicken into 1-inch chunks and chop the remaining parsley leaves. Stir the beans and vinegar into the pot and bring to a boil. Add the chicken and simmer for 2 minutes, or until heated through.

**SERVE** Ladle the soup into bowls and sprinkle with the chopped parsley.

*Makes 4 servings*

*Per serving: 286 calories, 31g protein, 31g carbohydrates, 5g fat, 1g saturated fat, 86mg cholesterol, 1,370mg sodium*

---

## Food Facts

### BEANS: A FOOD THAT HAS STOOD THE TEST OF TIME

Beans have been cultivated and enjoyed for over 4,000 years. No wonder, for they're tasty, good for you, and easy to prepare. Take your pick—there's a bean to satisfy every taste: pink, purple, black, white, green, speckled, large, small and everything in between.

Beans are so good for you because they are are rich in complex carbohydrates, providing lots of energy and fiber. Research shows that beans also help to lower your cholesterol. One serving of this soup provides about one-third of your daily fiber. Not only good for you, but delicious, too, beans are a winning combination!

# MAC 'N' DOUBLE CHEESE SOUP

*Prep* **5 MINUTES**      *Cook* **25 MINUTES**

*Turn that package of mac 'n' cheese dinner into a fast savory pot of stew. Another day, try adding a mix of Cheddar and Monterey Jack cheeses with a small minced jalapeño.*

| | |
|---|---|
| 3 | cups water |
| 2 | cups milk |
| 1 | package (14 ounces) macaroni and cheese dinner |
| 2 | cups frozen vegetable blend |
| 1 | package (8 ounces) classic melts shredded cheese (2 cups) |

**LET'S BEGIN** Combine the water and milk in a large saucepan and bring to a boil.

**STIR IT IN** Stir in the macaroni and vegetables and return to a boil. Reduce the heat and simmer for 12 to 14 minutes, until the macaroni is tender.

**SERVE** Blend in the shredded cheese and cheese sauce from the pouch. Cook, stirring, until the cheeses melt and are smooth.

*Makes 8 servings*

*Per serving: 282 calories, 13g protein, 22g carbohydrates, 16g fat, 8g saturated fat, 41mg cholesterol, 414mg sodium*

---

## Cook to Cook

### HOW CAN I TURN MY FAVORITE SOUPS INTO QUICK ONE-DISH MEALS?

❝ I start with my favorite *chicken noodle soup recipe* (or use canned if I'm in a hurry). I add extra protein, like extra *chunks of chicken,* and one or two *extra vegetables* such as diced fresh tomato and frozen peas.

Try adding cooked beans to vegetable soup. They're great and turn the soup into a meal. I use *black beans, pinto, or navy.* Just rinse, drain and toss into the pot.

I love to make a big pot of *vegetable soup,* because it helps me transform leftovers easily. One day I'll add *cooked bowties or spirals of pasta,* another day canned beans, still another, some pesto I buy on my way home. Then I top this with a slice of French bread, sprinkle with Parmesan, and broil.

Tomato soup is super filling when turned into *Pappa al Pomodoro* (bread-thickened tomato soup). Tear up pieces of *country bread* and simmer until the soup thickens. Then sprinkle pieces of *fresh basil* on top and drizzle with extra-virgin olive oil. *Bon Appetito!* ❞

Big "Bowl of Red"

# Big "Bowl of Red"

*Prep* **5 minutes**     *Cook* **43 minutes**

1¼   pounds lean ground beef

2    garlic cloves, minced

1½   tablespoons chili powder

1¾   cups hot or mild salsa

3    tablespoons naturally brewed lite soy sauce

1½   cups frozen green beans

1    can (15 ounces) black beans, rinsed and drained

Reduced-fat sour cream

Chopped fresh cilantro

*To Texans, chili is a "big bowl of red" — beef, beans, and spice.*

**LET'S BEGIN** Cook the beef with garlic and chili powder in a large saucepan over medium heat until brown. Stir in the salsa and 1 tablespoon of the soy sauce and bring to a boil.

**SIMMER LOW** Reduce the heat. Cover and simmer for 15 minutes. Stir in the green beans and simmer 15 minutes more. Stir in the black beans and cook for 5 minutes. Remove from the heat and stir in the remaining soy sauce. Serve with a dollop of sour cream and a sprinkling of cilantro.

*Makes 6 servings*

*Per serving: 310 calories, 23g protein, 17g carbohydrates, 17g fat, 7g saturated fat, 65mg cholesterol, 758mg sodium*

# Soul City Chili

*Prep* **10 minutes**     *Cook* **30 minutes**

1    pound Italian sausage

2    pounds lean ground beef

½    teaspoon each: seasoned salt and seasoned pepper

1    can (15¼ ounces) red kidney beans, undrained

1    can (14½ ounces) stewed tomatoes

2    cups water

2    packets (1.48) ounces each) chili seasoning

½    cup barbecue sauce

¾    cup dry red wine

Diced bell pepper and onion

*Down in the "Cities of Soul" through the South, folks expect their chili to taste like it has cooked for hours, even if it hasn't. Spicy sausages, fiery chili seasonings, and hot barbecue sauce do just that.*

**LET'S BEGIN** Remove the sausage casings. Cook the ground beef and sausage in a pot for 6 minutes, or until brown, breaking up the meat with the side of a spoon. Drain off the fat. Stir in the seasoned salt and pepper.

**FIX IT QUICK** Stir in the remaining ingredients except the diced bell pepper and onion. Bring to a boil over medium-high heat. Reduce the heat and simmer for 20 minutes.

**SERVE** Serve with bowls of bell pepper and onion.

*Makes 10 servings*

*Per serving: 472 calories, 27g protein, 17g carbohydrates, 31g fat, 11g saturated fat, 97mg cholesterol, 1,130mg sodium*

# AMERICAN CHILI POT

*Prep* **5 MINUTES**     *Cook* **25 MINUTES**

1   pound lean ground beef or ground turkey

1   can (15 ounces) red kidney beans, undrained

1   can (8 ounces) tomato sauce

1   tablespoon distilled white vinegar

2   tablespoons chili powder

2   tablespoons dried minced onion

1   teaspoon sugar (optional)

¼   teaspoon garlic salt

**Sliced scallions, sour cream, and shredded Cheddar cheese (optional)**

*Here it is—the all-American recipe for chili. Naturally, it has ground beef, kidney beans, tomato, and lots of chili powder. The best part: it's ready in half an hour.*

**LET'S BEGIN** Cook the meat in a large skillet over medium-high heat for 4 to 5 minutes, or until brown, breaking up the meat with the side of a spoon. Drain off the fat.

**STIR IT IN** Stir in the beans and their liquid, tomato sauce, vinegar, chili powder, onion, sugar, if using, and garlic salt. Bring to a boil, then immediately reduce the heat. Cover and simmer, stirring occasionally, for 15 to 20 minutes.

**SERVE** Spoon the chili into bowls and top with scallions, sour cream, and Cheddar, if desired.

*Makes 4 servings*

*Per serving: 395 calories, 28g protein, 25g carbohydrates, 20g fat, 8g saturated fat, 78mg cholesterol, 880mg sodium*

# TINA'S TACO SOUP

*Prep* **10 MINUTES**     *Cook* **19 MINUTES**

| | |
|---|---|
| 1 | **pound lean ground beef** |
| 1 | **tablespoon canola oil** |
| 1 | **medium onion, chopped** |
| ½ | **cup chopped celery** |
| 1 | **garlic clove, minced** |
| 1 | **jar (16 ounces) mild chunky salsa** |
| ½ | **package (16 ounces) frozen white and yellow corn blend** |
| 1 | **can (2¼ ounces) sliced ripe olives, drained** |
| 2 | **cans (14½ ounces each) beef broth** |
| 1 | **packet (1¼ ounces) taco seasoning** |

**Shredded Cheddar cheese, sour cream, and crumbled tortilla chips**

*This satisfying Tex-Mex soup is done in a flash! While it's bubbling away, cook up your favorite greens or toss a salad.*

**LET'S BEGIN** Cook the beef in a medium nonstick skillet for 6 minutes, or until brown, breaking up the meat with the side of a spoon. Drain off the fat and set aside.

**COOK IT QUICK** Heat the oil in a soup pot over medium-high heat. Sauté the onion, celery, and garlic for 3 minutes, or until the vegetables soften. Stir in the salsa, corn, olives, browned meat, broth, and taco seasoning and bring to a boil. Cover and reduce the heat to medium. Cook for 6 minutes, or until the vegetables are tender. Serve with Cheddar cheese, sour cream, and crumbled taco chips.

*Makes 4 to 6 servings*

*Per serving: 463 calories, 26g protein, 32g carbohydrates, 25g fat, 9g saturated fat, 78mg cholesterol, 2,653mg sodium*

## Food Facts

### THE VARIOUS VARIATIONS OF CHILI

Where you're eating a "bowl of red" depends on what's in the chili pot. If you're in Texas, your chili con carne (with meat) will be made with cubes of beef chuck and lots of smoky ancho chili powder.

Chili in Cincinnati, on the other hand, is like none other. In fact, Cincinnatians are chili fanatics! This city's Two-Way Chili is spiced with cinnamon and other Middle Eastern spices and served over spaghetti. Three-Way is then topped with shredded Cheddar, Four-Way is also shattered with chopped onion, and Five-Way is additionally crowned with red kidney beans. It's traditionally served with two hot dogs sprinkled with more cheese.

If you're having chili in New Mexico, it may be made with lamb or mutton instead of beef.

# Italian Cupboard Stew
*Prep* **5 minutes**    *Cook* **24 minutes**

| | |
|---|---|
| 2 | boneless pork chops |
| 1 | tablespoon vegetable oil |
| 2 | cans (14½ ounces each) chicken broth |
| 1 | can (15 ounces) cannellini or great Northern beans, drained |
| 1 | can (15 ounces) chopped tomatoes, undrained |
| 2 | tablespoons dried minced onion |
| 8 | ounces fresh spinach leaves, torn |

*The Italians are famous for their innovative ways with flavors and ingredients. Here, a super-quick supper that's easy to double.*

**LET'S BEGIN**  Cut the pork into 1-inch cubes. Heat the oil in a large saucepot. Sauté the pork over medium-high heat for 5 minutes or until brown all over.  Stir in all of the remaining ingredients except the spinach and bring to a boil,

**SIMMER LOW**  Reduce the heat and simmer for 15 minutes. Stir in the spinach and cook 2 minutes more. Top with freshly grated Parmesan cheese, if you wish.

*Makes 4 servings*

*Per serving: 240 calories, 22g protein, 27g carbohydrates, 5g fat, 2g saturated fat, 35mg cholesterol, 620mg sodium*

# Ham 'n' Cheese Kettle
*Prep* **15 minutes**    *Cook* **27 minutes**

| | |
|---|---|
| 8 | small new red potatoes |
| 8 | slices American cheese |
| 1 | tablespoon butter |
| ½ | cup chopped onion |
| 2 | tablespoons flour |
| ½ | cup chopped red bell pepper |
| 1 | can (14½ ounces) chicken broth |
| ½ | teaspoon dried sage |
| ¼ | teaspoon ground pepper |
| ½ | cup frozen peas |
| 2 | cups cubed baked ham |

*All the popular fixings of the beloved American ham 'n' cheese sandwich inside a soup pot. Add potatoes and peas, and it's dinner!*

**LET'S BEGIN**  Cut the potatoes into 6 wedges each. Cut cheese into thin strips. Melt the butter in a large saucepot over medium heat. Add the onion and sauté them for 3 to 4 minutes. Stir in the flour until well mixed.

**BUBBLE & BOIL**  Add the red bell pepper, broth, potatoes, sage, and pepper. Cover and cook for 15 to 20 minutes, until the potatoes are tender. Stir in all of the remaining ingredients. Cook for 8 minutes, or until hot.

*Makes 6 servings*

*Per serving: 274 calories, 20g protein, 16g carbohydrates, 14g fat, 8g saturated fat, 52mg cholesterol, 1,548mg sodium*

*Italian Cupboard Stew*

# SLOW-COOKER TUSCAN BEEF STEW

*Prep* **10 MINUTES**      *Slow-cook* **4¼ HOURS**

| | |
|---|---|
| 2 | pounds beef stew meat, cut into 1-inch chunks |
| 3 | large carrots, cut into 1-inch chunks |
| 1 | can (14½ ounces) diced Italian-style tomatoes |
| 1 | can (10¾ ounces) tomato soup |
| 1 | can condensed beef broth |
| ½ | cup dry red wine or water |
| 1 | teaspoon dried Italian seasoning, crushed |
| ½ | teaspoon garlic powder |
| 2 | cans (15 ounces each) white kidney beans, rinsed and drained |

*Toss together the ingredients for this long-simmered stew in the morning and forget about it until 10 minutes before serving. Then, turn up the heat, stir in the beans, and it's done!*

**LET'S BEGIN** Combine all of the ingredients, except the beans, in a 3½-quart slow cooker.

**SIMMER LOW** Cover the cooker and cook on High for 4 or 5 hours or on Low for 8 or 9 hours.

**STIR IT IN** Stir in the beans. Turn the heat to High and cook 10 minutes longer, or until heated through

*Makes 8 servings*

*Per serving: 306 calories, 31g protein, 28g carbohydrates, 6g fat, 2g saturated fat, 70mg cholesterol, 1,090mg sodium*

---

## Food Facts

### SAVE DOUGH WHEN BUYING BEEF

To save the most money when buying beef, always buy a hunk of beef and cut it into chunks for stew yourself. Supermarkets charge you more per pound for cutting up meat. Plus, the meat they cut into chunks is not always from the best cut of beef for stewing.

Tip: Cut the meat into ¾-inch cubes (instead of the larger 1-inch ones usually sold in the market). They'll cook quicker in the pot.

For the stew pot, buy a nice piece of chuck (such as blade pot roast or brisket). It has lots of delicious flavor and good texture,

which is brought out by long, slow, moist cooking. This cut simmers up nice and moist and has a richer beefy flavor than any other cut. You can also buy bottom round, rump, or shank, but these cuts are lower in fat and can turn "dry" in the stewing pot.

_SuperQuick_

# TEXAS BEEF STEW

_Prep_ **10 MINUTES**      _Cook_ **10 MINUTES**

1    can (14½ ounces) whole new potatoes

1    pound lean ground beef

1    small onion, chopped

1    can (28 ounces) crushed tomatoes with roasted garlic

1½  cups frozen broccoli, cauliflower, and carrots

1    can (4½ ounces) chopped green chilies, drained

1    cup frozen corn kernels

½    cup water

_You just have to chop one small onion for this fast stew. Brown it with the beef, mix with other ingredients, and simmer 5 minutes._

**LET'S BEGIN** Halve the potatoes, reserving their liquid. Combine the beef and onion in a soup pot and cook over medium-high heat until the beef is brown, breaking it up with the side of a spoon. Add tomatoes, vegetables, potatoes with their liquid, chilies, water, and corn and bring to a boil.

**SIMMER LOW** Cover and simmer for 5 minutes, or until heated through. Serve over cooked rice, if you wish.

_Makes 4 servings_

_Per serving: 425 calories, 27g protein, 36g carbohydrates, 20g fat, 8g saturated fat, 78mg cholesterol, 738mg sodium_

# MIDWESTERN CHEESE POT

_Prep_ **15 MINUTES**      _Cook_ **30 MINUTES**

2    cups finely chopped potatoes

½    cup each: chopped carrots and celery

¼    cup chopped onion

2    cups water

1    teaspoon salt

¼    cup butter or margarine

¼    cup all-purpose flour

2    cups milk

1¼  cups (5 ounces) shredded sharp Cheddar cheese

1    can (17 ounces) cream-style corn

_In the Midwest, where corn grows for miles and farms are numerous, corn and cheese are often used in one-dish meals._

**LET'S BEGIN** Bring the potatoes, carrots, celery, onion, water, and salt to a boil in a soup pot. Reduce heat to low. Cover and simmer for 10 minutes. Remove from heat. Do not drain.

**BUBBLE & STIR** Melt butter in a large saucepan over low heat. Stir in the flour and cook for 2 minutes or until bubbly. Blend in the milk and cook, stirring constantly, until it boils and thickens. Reduce heat to low and simmer for 5 minutes.

**STIR IT IN** Stir in the cheese and cook until melted. Add the undrained vegetables and corn. Cook until hot.

_Makes 8 servings_

_Per serving: 260 calories, 9g protein, 26g carbohydrates, 14g fat, 9g saturated fat, 44mg cholesterol, 677mg sodium_

# BEEFY MEAL-IN-A-POT

*Prep* **5 MINUTES**     *Cook* **19 MINUTES**

1   **pound ground beef**

3   **garlic cloves, minced**

1   **package (16 ounces) Italian-style frozen vegetables**

2   **cups southern-style hash brown potatoes**

1   **jar (14 ounces) marinara sauce**

1   **can (10½ ounces) condensed beef broth**

3   **tablespoons Worcestershire sauce**

**Garlic bread (optional)**

*Make fast 'n' fabulous garlic bread: Split and toast a baguette. Top with sautéed minced garlic and sprinkle with Kosher salt. Yum!*

**LET'S BEGIN**  Cook the beef and garlic in a soup pot for 6 minutes, or until brown, breaking up the meat with the side of a spoon. Drain off the fat.

**STIR IT IN**  Add the remaining ingredients to the pot and bring to a boil. Reduce the heat. Cover and simmer, stirring occasionally, for 10 minutes, or until the vegetables are crisp-tender. Serve with garlic bread, if you wish.

*Makes 4 servings*

*Per serving: 590 calories, 31g protein, 42g carbohydrates, 34g fat, 12g saturated fat, 78mg cholesterol, 1,022mg sodium*

# QUICK & EASY BEEF STEW

*Prep* **5 MINUTES**    *Cook* **22 MINUTES**

2    pounds boneless sirloin steak, cut into ¾-inch chunks

3    tablespoons flour

1    tablespoon oil

1    package (24 ounces) frozen mixed vegetables or 5 cups cut-up fresh vegetables

3    cups water

1    package beef stew seasoning

*This stew cooks very quickly, so you'll need a tender cut of meat. Sirloin, round tip, tri-tip, or chuck-eye will all hit the mark.*

**LET'S BEGIN**  Cut beef into ¾-inch cubes and coat with flour.  Sauté beef in oil in a large skillet or Dutch oven over medium-high heat for 6 minutes, or until brown. Drain.

**STIR IT IN**  Stir the vegetables, water, and beef seasoning into the pan and bring to a boil. Reduce heat, cover, and simmer for 15 minutes, or until the vegetables are tender.

*Makes 8 servings*

*Per serving: 384 calories, 24g protein, 17g carbohydrates, 25g fat, 9g saturated fat, 77mg cholesterol, 527mg sodium*

# SMOKY PASTA & BEAN SOUP

*Prep* **10 MINUTES** *Cook* **43 MINUTES**

| | |
|---|---|
| 6 | slices bacon, diced |
| 1 | small onion, finely chopped |
| 1 | celery rib, finely chopped |
| 1 | medium carrot, peeled and grated |
| 2 | garlic cloves, minced |
| ⅛ | teaspoon crushed hot red pepper flakes |
| 2 | cups canned crushed tomatoes |
| 2½ | cups drained canned white beans |
| 6 | cups chicken broth |
| ¾ | cup macaroni or other small pasta shape |

Freshly grated Parmesan cheese (optional)

*Here are three favorites all in one pot—bacon, beans, and pasta. Just sauté a few ingredients fast, then let the pot simmer on its own.*

**LET'S BEGIN** Sauté the bacon in a large skillet over medium-high heat for 5 minutes. Add the onion, celery, carrot, garlic, and pepper flakes and sauté for 10 minutes, or until the vegetables are tender.

**STIR IT IN** Add the tomatoes and cook for 10 minutes, stirring occasionally. Stir in the beans.

**BUBBLE & BOIL** Pour in the broth and bring to a gentle boil. Add the macaroni and simmer for 15 minutes, or until the pasta is al dente. Top with Parmesan cheese, if you wish.

*Makes 8 servings*
*Per serving: 180 calories, 10g protein, 26g carbohydrates, 6g fat, 1g saturated fat, 10mg cholesterol, 1,310mg sodium*

---

## Cooking Basics

### FAST WAYS TO ADD "HOT" TO THE POT

Peppers are an instant way to add a "spice of hot" to your soup. Here's how some match up in heat—from mild to wild.
1. Sweet or roasted bell peppers—the mildest
2. Hungarian cherry—bright red, round, medium-hot
3. Anaheim—medium green, long, with a bite
4. Poblano chili—dark green, triangular, with snap

5. Pepperoncini—wrinkled Tuscan peppers and medium-hot
6. Jalapeño—dark green, small, with hot seeds
7. Serrano chile—popular in Mexican dishes
8. Thai chile—red chile popular in Asian dishes
9. Scotch bonnet chile—one of the hottest chiles
10. Habanero—popular in Yucatán dishes; watch out!

# WHITE BEAN, CHICKEN, & CHILI POT

*Prep* **15 MINUTES**    *Cook* **2 HOURS**

4    boneless, skinless chicken breast halves (1¼ pounds)

5    cans (14½ ounces each) chicken broth

½    cup water

1    pound dried white beans

½    cup chopped onion

¾    teaspoon garlic powder with parsley

½    teaspoon dried basil

1    can (4 ounces) diced green chilies, drained

2    teaspoons each ground cumin, dried oregano, and chopped fresh cilantro

1    teaspoon seasoned salt

½    teaspoon lemon pepper

Shredded Cheddar cheese and chopped scallions (optional)

*Make this recipe super-fast by substituting canned beans for the homecooked ones. Use 2 cans (14½ ounces each) Great Northern or white kidney cannellini beans for the dried ones.*

**LET'S BEGIN** Cook and dice the chicken. Combine the broth, water, beans, onion, garlic powder with parsley, and basil in a soup pot and bring to a boil.

**SIMMER LOW** Reduce heat. Cover and simmer for 1½ hours, or until the beans are tender. Stir in all of the remaining ingredients except the Cheddar and scallions. Cover and cook, stirring occasionally, for 20 minutes longer.

**SERVE** Ladle the soup into bowls and sprinkle with Cheddar and scallions, if you wish.

*Makes 6 servings*

*Per serving: 426 calories, 47g protein, 50g carbohydrates, 4g fat, 1g saturated fat, 55mg cholesterol, 1,516mg sodium*

## Cooking Basics

### TURN THIS CHILI INTO A FRENCH STEW!

The test of a good recipe is how flexible it is. With a few quick switches to some key ingredients, this White Bean, Chicken & Chili Pot can be made into a country French stew. Substitute 3 cups baked ham for the chicken and 1 cup dry white wine for 1 cup of the chicken broth. Add 1 cup sliced carrots with the chicken. Omit the green chilies. Top with snipped chives instead of the Cheddar and scallions.

# SHRIMP CREOLE

*Prep* **15 MINUTES**     *Cook* **23 MINUTES**

1½   **cups raw small shrimp**

1   **package (16 ounces) frozen broccoli, cauliflower, and red pepper blend**

1   **can (14½ ounces) diced tomatoes**

1½   **teaspoons salt**

1   **to 2 teaspoons hot pepper sauce**

1   **teaspoon vegetable oil**

**Hot cooked white rice**

*Here's a meal in a pot that's typically Creole: shrimp from the Gulf, fresh tomatoes, rice, and, of course, hot pepper sauce. Speed up this dish by buying shrimp that has already been shelled and deveined.*

**LET'S BEGIN** Peel and devein the shrimp Combine all of the ingredients in a soup pot. Cover and bring to a boil.

**SIMMER LOW** Reduce the heat and simmer for 20 minutes, or until the shrimp are opaque throughout. Ladle the stew into large bowls and serve rice alongside.

*Makes 4 servings*

*Per serving: 117 calories, 13g protein, 10g carbohydrates, 2g fat, 0g saturated fat, 73mg cholesterol, 1,259mg sodium*

---

*SuperQuick*

# WEEKDAY SEAFOOD CHOWDER

*Prep* **15 MINUTES**     *Cook* **7 MINUTES**

2   **cans (6½ ounces each) clams, drained (reserve liquid)**

½   **pound raw medium shrimp**

1   **jar (26 ounces) marinara & burgundy wine pasta sauce**

1   **can (14½ ounces) sliced potatoes, drained**

1   **cup frozen green peas**

**Salt and ground black pepper (optional)**

**Grated Parmesan cheese**

*Seafood tonight! Toss clams and shrimp into this fast chowder pot one day, then try another combination of scallops and shrimp another.*

**LET'S BEGIN** Add enough water to the reserved clam liquid to equal 1¾ cups and pour into a large saucepan. Peel and devein the shrimp. Add the shrimp to pot with all the remaining ingredients.

**INTO THE PAN** Cook over medium-high heat, stirring occasionally, for 7 minutes or until shrimp turn pink. Season, if desired, with salt and ground black pepper and garnish with grated Parmesan cheese.

*Makes 8 servings*

*Per serving: 210 calories, 21g protein, 21g carbohydrates, 4g fat, 1g saturated fat, 75mg cholesterol, 606mg sodium*

# HOPPIN' JOHN SOUP

*Prep* **10 MINUTES**　　*Cook* **20 MINUTES**

| | |
|---|---|
| 4 | slices bacon, chopped |
| 1 | large onion, chopped |
| 2 | garlic cloves, minced |
| 2 | cans (15 ounces each) black-eyed peas, undrained |
| 1 | can (14½ ounces) reduced-sodium chicken broth |
| ½ | cup water |
| 3 | to 4 tablespoons cayenne pepper sauce |
| 1 | teaspoon dried thyme |
| 1 | bay leaf |
| 2 | cups cooked long-grain white rice |
| 2 | tablespoons finely chopped fresh parsley |

*New Year's Day dinner in the South just wouldn't be the same without a steaming bowl of Hoppin' John. Traditionally, this dish simmers for hours. Ours is so speedy, you'll be serving it year round.*

**LET'S BEGIN** Cook the bacon, onion, and garlic in a large saucepan over medium-high heat for 5 minutes, or until the vegetables are soft.

**SIMMER LOW** Add the black-eyed peas with their liquid, the broth, water, pepper sauce, thyme, and bay leaf and bring to a boil. Reduce the heat. Cover the pot and simmer for 15 minutes, stirring occasionally. Remove the bay leaf.

**SERVE** Combine the rice and the parsley in a medium bowl. Spoon the rice into soup bowls and ladle in the soup.

*Makes 6 servings*

*Per serving: 228 calories, 11g protein, 37g carbohydrates, 4g fat, 1g saturated fat, 5g cholesterol, 717mg sodium*

---

## Food Facts

### HOPPIN' JOHN—SOUTHERN GOOD-LUCK CHARM

Most southerners agree: Hoppin' John brings you good luck, provided you eat it on New Year's Day. In many homes, the big pot of cowpeas (black-eyed peas) with fat-back (pork), rice, and plenty of seasonings and spice often simmers throughout the year, but always on New Year's Day.

As some tales go, the name relates to the custom of inviting folks for supper with the offer of "Hop in, John." Other stories connect the name with the old ritual that children "hopped once around the table" before eating the dish.

Back in the 1600s, the French Huguenots settled in the low country of the Carolinas, bringing with them their beloved French rice pilafs. Hoppin' John evolved from the blending of their cooking with that of the African-Americans and the local ingredients.

# HAM & BARLEY CREAM SOUP

Prep **5 MINUTES**    Cook **25 MINUTES**

*This is comfort food at its fastest, easiest, and best. Quick-cooking barley cuts down on the cooking time, while tender strips of ham add good smoky flavor.*

| | |
|---|---|
| ¼ | cup butter or margarine |
| ¼ | cup finely chopped onion |
| 1 | cup quick-cooking barley |
| 1 | thick slice ham (6 ounces), cut into strips |
| 5½ | cups water |
| 5½ | teaspoons chicken-flavored instant bouillon granules |
| ¼ | teaspoon poultry seasoning |
| ¼ | teaspoon ground white pepper |
| 1 | cup heavy cream |
| 1 | cup frozen tiny peas, thawed |
| 1 | cup grated Parmesan cheese |
| | Ground nutmeg |

**LET'S BEGIN** Melt the butter in a large saucepan over medium heat. Sauté the onion for 3 to 5 minutes, until soft. Stir in the barley and cook, stirring, until it turns light golden. Stir in the ham, water, bouillon granules, poultry seasoning, and white pepper and bring to a boil.

**SIMMER LOW** Reduce the heat. Cover the pot and simmer for 15 minutes, or until the barley is tender. Stir in the cream and peas and cook for 3 minutes, or until heated through. Serve with Parmesan and a generous sprinkling of nutmeg.

### Makes 8 servings

*Per serving: 326 calories, 12g protein, 19g carbohydrates, 23g fat, 13g saturated fat, 77mg cholesterol, 1,168mg sodium*

---

## On the Menu

*Gather 'round the fire on a chilly day...warm up with this soul-satisfying meal.*

Ham & Barley Cream Soup

Whole-grain Rolls
and Cheddar

Green Beans with
Toasted Walnuts

Pineapple
Upside-Down Cake
Vanilla Whipped Cream

# PORK & PEPPER STEW

*Prep* **15 MINUTES**     *Cook* **24 MINUTES**

| | |
|---|---|
| 3 | boneless pork chops |
| 2 | teaspoons vegetable oil |
| 1 | medium onion, chopped |
| 2 | garlic cloves, minced |
| 1 | can (14½ ounces) diced tomatoes, undrained |
| 8 | small red new potatoes (1 pound), quartered |
| 2 | bell peppers (red or green), cut into bite-size ½-inch-wide strips |
| 1¼ | cups beef broth |
| 2 | teaspoons dried marjoram, crumbled |
| ½ | teaspoon salt |
| ¼ | teaspoon pepper |
| 2 | tablespoons flour |
| ¼ | cup chopped parsley |

*Here's meat and potatoes, true American style—all in one pot. It's all here, the chunks of juicy pork, the new red potatoes, onions, peppers, and just the right seasonings. All you need are big appetites!*

**LET'S BEGIN**  Cut the pork into ¾-inch cubes. Heat the oil in a Dutch oven over medium-high heat. Sauté the onion and garlic until tender but not brown.

**INTO THE PAN**  Add the pork to the Dutch oven and stir-fry for 2 to 3 minutes, or until brown. Stir in the tomatoes, potatoes, peppers, 1 cup of beef broth, the marjoram, salt, and pepper. Bring to a boil. Reduce the heat to low.

**SIMMER LOW**  Cover and simmer for about 15 minutes or until the pork and potatoes are tender. Dissolve the flour in the remaining ¼ cup beef broth, then stir it into the stew. Increase the heat to medium and stir constantly until the mixture thickens. Stir in the parsley.

*Makes 4 servings*
*Per serving: 341 calories, 21g protein, 35g carbohydrates, 13g fat, 4g saturated fat, 45mg cholesterol, 909mg sodium*

---

## Food Facts

### BOOST UP THE NUTRITION

**Add a good-for-you food** to the soup pot and quickly boost up the nutrition in every bite.

**Pop in Pasta**—Toss in some very thin noodles, a handful of rice, or some orzo. You'll be adding complex carbohydrates (extra energy!) at the same time.

**Grab some grains**—Stir in some brown rice, barley, or whole-wheat pasta and increase the fiber in the pot (good for digestion).

**Slice a Carrot**—Just slice up one carrot and throw it into the pot. You'll boost up the vitamin A fast (great for keeping eyes healthy).

**Chop a Tomato**—Stir in a chopped tomato, and you'll be adding vitamin C (good for your immune system).

**Go for the Leaf**—Tear up fresh spinach or other leafy vegetables and throw them into the pot. They increase folic acid in your diet.

# ZESTY ITALIAN SOUP

*Prep* **15 MINUTES**     *Cook* **40 MINUTES**

*Leave it to the Italians to know how to create wonderful soups with tomatoes, vegetables, pepperoni, and cheese. And chances are, you have most of these ingredients already at hand.*

| | |
|---|---|
| 1 | large baking potato |
| 5 | cups water |
| ⅔ | cup chopped onion |
| ½ | cup chopped celery |
| 1 | large carrot, diced |
| 6 | chicken bouillon cubes |
| 1 | can (14½ ounces) diced tomatoes |
| 1 | can (8 ounces) tomato sauce |
| 2 | tablespoons chopped parsley |
| 1 | garlic clove, minced |
| ¼ | teaspoon dried oregano |
| 1 | cup diced pepperoni |
| 2 | tablespoons shredded Parmesan cheese |

**LET'S BEGIN**  Peel and dice the potato and place in a large soup pot. Add the next 5 ingredients and bring to a boil over high heat.

**SIMMER LOW**  Reduce the heat. Cover and simmer for 15 minutes. Add all of the remaining ingredients except the pepperoni and cheese. Cover and simmer 20 minutes longer, or until the potato is tender.

**STIR IT IN**  Stir in the pepperoni and cheese and cook, stirring, until heated through and bubbling.

*Makes 8 servings*
*Per serving: 132 calories, 6g protein, 13g carbohydrates, 7g fat, 3g saturated fat, 12mg cholesterol, 1,431mg sodium*

# ITALIAN SAUSAGE STEW

*Prep* **5 MINUTES**     *Cook* **10 MINUTES**

2   boxes (10 ounces) frozen Italian-style vegetables

2   cans (14 ounces each) beef broth

1   pound sweet or hot Italian sausage links, casings removed

1   can (8 ounces) tomato sauce

*Here's a stew pot from just four ingredients—nothing could be easier or faster. The best part: the spicy sausage flavors the whole pot.*

**LET'S BEGIN** Combine the vegetables and broth in a soup pot and bring to a boil.

**SIMMER LOW** Reduce heat and cover the pot. Simmer for 7 to 10 minutes, until the vegetables are tender.

**BROWN IT** Meanwhile, cook the sausages in a medium skillet for 6 minutes, or until brown, breaking them up with the side of a spoon. Drain off the fat. Stir the sausages into the stew pot and cook for 2 minutes longer, or until heated through.

*Makes 4 servings*

*Per serving: 472 calories, 30g protein, 18g carbohydrates, 33g fat, 16g saturated fat, 77mg cholesterol, 2,534mg sodium*

---

## Cook to Cook

### CAN I MAKE DIFFERENT SUPPERS FROM THIS SAUSAGE STEW?

❝ I like to throw *2 cups of cooked bowtie pasta* and a cup of drained cannellini beans into this pot of Italian Sausage Stew. Toss it in during the last few minutes of cooking, along with the sausage. Be sure to sprinkle the stew with freshly grated Parmesan before taking it to the table.

Toss *fresh cheese tortellini* into this sausage stew for a very hearty meal. Add 2 cups of the refrigerated pasta to the pot during the last 5 minutes of cooking.

Another time, toss in *2 cups of sliced fresh mushrooms* with the frozen vegetables. After the stew is done, ladle it into soup crocks, top with a slice of Mozzarella cheese, and pop under the broiler a minute to melt. ❞

# PIEDMONT PORK STEW
*Prep* **10 MINUTES**    *Cook* **18 MINUTES**

| | |
|---|---|
| 1 | teaspoon oil |
| 1 | pound boneless pork loin, cut into ¾-inch cubes |
| 1 | medium onion, coarsely chopped |
| 2 | carrots, sliced |
| 8 | ounces mushrooms, coarsely chopped |
| 1 | can (8 ounces) tomato sauce |
| 1 | cup dry red wine |
| 1 | teaspoon dried thyme |
| 1 | teaspoon dried oregano |
| ¼ | teaspoon cinnamon |
| ¼ | teaspoon salt |
| ½ | cup dark raisins |

*In the Piedmont mountain area, they like their stews hearty, hot, and full of flavor. Make a double batch and freeze half.*

**LET'S BEGIN** Heat the oil in a large saucepot over medium-high heat. Sauté the pork for 3 to 4 minutes, or until brown.

**INTO THE PAN** Add all of the remaining ingredients and bring to a boil.

**SIMMER LOW** Reduce the heat and simmer for 15 to 20 minutes, or until the pork and vegetables are tender.

*Makes 6 servings*
*Per serving: 220 calories, 18g protein, 19g carbohydrates, 5g fat, 1g saturated fat, 45mg cholesterol, 710mg sodium*

# Toasty Tomato & Chicken Stew

*Prep* **10 MINUTES**     *Cook* **30 MINUTES**

2   cans (14½ ounces each) tomatoes with chilies

1   cup shredded roasted chicken

1   small yellow onion, chopped

2½   cups fresh bread cubes

½   teaspoon salt

2   tablespoons butter

½   cup Parmesan cheese

*What a simple way to serve supper! Toss five ingredients into a baker, dot with butter, push into the oven, and walk away. Nothing could be simpler—or tastier.*

**LET'S BEGIN** Preheat oven to 375°F. Combine tomatoes, chicken, onion, bread cubes, and salt in a medium bowl.

**INTO THE OVEN** Spoon the mixture into a greased 8 x 8-inch casserole and dot with butter. Bake for 20 minutes. Sprinkle with Parmesan cheese and bake 10 minutes longer.

> *Makes 4 servings*
>
> *Per serving: 292 calories, 18g protein, 26g carbohydrates, 12g fat, 7g saturated fat, 56mg cholesterol, 1,017mg sodium*

# Country Cupboard Kettle

*Prep* **10 MINUTES**     *Cook* **35 MINUTES**

½   pound boneless pork loin or 2 boneless pork chops

1   teaspoon oil

4   cups water

1   can (28 ounces) crushed tomatoes

1   cup thinly sliced carrots

1   cup sliced potatoes

1   envelope (4 ounces) dry onion soup mix

2   tablespoons sugar

¼   teaspoon dried oregano

Dash red pepper sauce

Black pepper to taste

*In a busy country kitchen, the soup kettle's often simmering away on the stove. This one-pot soup is typical one-pot cooking: toss into the pot and forget it until it's done.*

**LET'S BEGIN** Cut the pork into ½-inch cubes. Heat the oil in a Dutch oven over medium-high heat and brown the pork.

**BUBBLE IT UP** Add all of the remaining ingredients and bring to a boil.

**SIMMER LOW** Reduce the heat. Cover and simmer gently for 30 to 45 minutes.

> *Makes 6 servings*
>
> *Per serving: 204 calories, 13g protein, 31g carbohydrates, 4g fat, 1g saturated fat, 24mg cholesterol, 1,890mg sodium*

*Toasty Tomato & Chicken Stew*

*Brunswick Stew, page 124*

# On the Weekend

It's the weekend—and that means the perfect time to simmer up a homemade soup stock and make everyone's favorite noodle soup. For a change of pace, try updating it with fun-shaped pasta. Or try one of our hearty stews—there are lots of them. From the classic Irish Lamb Stew to the traditional Brunswick Stew from colonial times and a hearty white bean. All take less than a half hour to start, so you can then walk away and let them simmer on their own. When friends gather, fill the soup pot with French Onion, Kickin' Texas Chili, or an elegant Swiss & Crab Mornay. All use quick-cooking products and tips to cut the fixing time. Plus, many of our recipes make enough for leftovers, too.

# BEST-EVER CHICKEN NOODLE

*Prep* **15 MINUTES**    *Cook* **1¾ HOURS**

| | |
|---|---|
| 1 | chicken (about 3 pounds) |
| 10 | cups cold water |
| 4 | large carrots |
| 2 | large onions |
| 2 | celery ribs, quartered |
| 6 | garlic cloves, minced |
| 2 | fresh thyme sprigs or ½ teaspoon dried |
| 1½ | teaspoons kosher salt |
| 1 | teaspoon whole black peppercorns |
| 1 | cup small pasta |
| 1 | cup frozen peas, thawed |
| | Salt and ground black pepper |
| 2 | tablespoons snipped fresh dill |
| 2 | tablespoons chopped fresh parsley |

*Chicken noodle soup is as American as football and franks. Our recipe is the real thing! Use noodles for the pasta, if you wish.*

**LET'S BEGIN** To make chicken broth, place the chicken (remove the neck and giblets) in a large soup pot. Add the next 8 ingredients. Cover and bring to a boil over high heat, occasionally skimming the foam and fat.

**SIMMER LOW** Reduce heat. Simmer, partially covered, for 1½ hours, adding more water to keep chicken covered if needed. Meanwhile, cook pasta according to package directions. Transfer chicken, onions, and carrots to a platter. Strain broth and return to the pot. Cut chicken into bite-size pieces. Discard bones and skin. Cshop carrots and onions.

**BUBBLE & STIR** Bring the broth to a rolling boil over high heat. Return the chicken, onions, and carrots to the broth along with pasta and peas. Reduce heat and simmer for 15 minutes, or until heated through. Season with salt and pepper, ladle into bowls, and sprinkle with the dill and parsley.

*Makes 8 servings*
*Per serving: 321 calories, 35g protein, 27g carbohydrates, 7g fat, 2g saturated fat, 82mg cholesterol, 975mg sodium*

---

## Cooking Basics

### CHOP LARGE...CHOP FAST

Unless you are using one of our *SuperQuick* recipes, fast-cut veggies into ¾-inch thick pieces and meats into 1-inch bite-size chunks for the soup and stew pot. Dicing them smaller takes longer, and they're likely to fall apart in the pot as they cook.

*SuperQuick* recipes suggest cutting ingredients into smaller pieces: ½-inch-sthick slices for vegetables and ¾-inch pieces for meat. Since they are in the pot for less time, they'll cook fast and stay together.

# BISCUIT-TOPPED HAMBURGER STEW

*Prep* **15 MINUTES**      *Cook/Bake* **37 MINUTES**

*This dish combines all the fixings of a great hamburger, simmered in a pot of stew. Top it off in an instant with biscuits out of a can and bake it up until bubbly and brown. Watch it disappear fast.*

| | |
|---|---|
| 1 | pound lean ground beef |
| ½ | cup coarsely chopped onion |
| 1 | can (14½ ounces) diced tomatoes, undrained |
| 1 | jar (12 ounces) home-style beef gravy |
| 1½ | cups diced peeled potatoes |
| 1 | cup carrot strips (1x¼x¼-inch) |
| 1 | cup frozen cut green beans |
| ¼ | teaspoon ground black pepper |
| 1 | can (6 ounces) refrigerated biscuits |

**LET'S BEGIN** Preheat the oven to 375°F. Spray a large skillet with nonstick cooking spray and heat over medium-high heat until hot. Sauté the ground beef and onion for about 7 minutes, or until the beef is cooked throughout.

**MIX IT UP** Stir in all of the remaining ingredients except the biscuits and bring to a boil Reduce heat to medium-low. Cover and simmer, stirring occasionally, for 10 to 15 minutes.

**INTO THE OVEN** Spoon the stew into an ungreased 8-inch square (2-quart) or an oval (2½-quart) baking dish. Separate the dough into 5 biscuits and cut each in half. Arrange, cut side down, around the outside edge of the hot stew. Bake at 375°F for 20 minutes, or until stew is bubbly and biscuits are deep golden brown.

*Makes 4 servings*

*Per serving: 503 calories, 30g protein, 44g carbohydrates, 23g fat, 9g saturated fat, 81mg cholesterol, 1,258mg sodium*

# CARIBBEAN ONE-POT STEW

*Prep* **15 MINUTES**     *Cook* **32 MINUTES**

| | |
|---|---|
| 1 | pound pork loin |
| 1 | pound sweet potatoes |
| 2 | tablespoons olive oil |
| 2 | tablespoons minced ginger |
| 3 | garlic cloves, minced |
| ¼ | jalapeño, minced |
| 1 | cup each: diced celery, green bell pepper, and onion |
| 1 | teaspoon ground cumin |
| ½ | teaspoon salt |
| ¼ | teaspoon ground black pepper |
| 3 | cans (16 ounces each) dark red kidney beans, rinsed and drained |
| 1 | can (14.5 ounces) diced tomatoes |
| 1 | can (14.5 ounces) chicken broth |

*Here's a stewpot like you'll find in the Caribbean—with plenty of pork and vegetables. Let your microwave help you fix it fast.*

**LET'S BEGIN** Trim pork and cut into ½-inch cubes. Prick sweet potatoes with a fork and microwave on High for 6 to 8 minutes, until tender. Peel and cut into ½-inch cubes.

**INTO THE POT** Meanwhile, heat oil in a large stockpot and sauté ginger, garlic, and jalapeño for 2 minutes. Add celery, bell pepper, and onion and cook 5 minutes more, or until crisp-tender. Season pork with cumin, salt, and pepper. Push vegetables to one side and add pork, browning on all sides. Add beans, tomatoes, broth, and potatoes. Bring to a boil.

**SIMMER LOW** Reduce heat and simmer for 25 to 30 minutes, or until pork is tender. Taste and adjust seasonings. Serve with hot sauce and fresh pineapple salsa, if desired.

*Makes 8 servings*

*Per serving: 310 calories, 22g protein, 40g carbohydrates, 7g fat, 2g saturated fat, 37mg cholesterol, 855mg sodium*

# BRUNSWICK STEW

*Prep* **20 MINUTES**　　　*Cook* **1¼ HOUR**

**Roasted garlic (see recipe)**

| | |
|---|---|
| 1 | **each: red, yellow, and orange bell pepper** |
| 24 | **pearl onions** |
| 3 | **medium all-purpose potatoes** |
| 2 | **ears corn** |
| 1 | **small yellow squash** |
| 3 | **pounds chicken pieces** |
| ⅛ | **teaspoon each: garlic salt and dried oregano** |
| ½ | **teaspoon ground black pepper** |
| 2 | **tablespoons olive oil** |
| 1 | **can (14½ ounces) whole tomatoes, chopped, juice reserved** |
| 1 | **can (14½ ounces) unsalted chicken broth** |
| 1 | **tablespoon fresh sage, chopped or 2 teaspoons dried, crumbled** |
| ½ | **teaspoon salt** |

*Traditionally, Brunswick stew contained squirrel and lots of onions. Chicken and a colorful array of vegetables is now preferred. To save time, use canned diced tomatoes and precut bell peppers.*

**LET'S BEGIN** Roast a head of garlic. Cut the bell peppers into chunks. Trim and peel the onions. Peel and cut the potatoes into 1-inch chunks. Cut the corn into 2-inch lengths and the squash into ½-inch-thick slices.

**INTO THE POT** Season the chicken with the garlic salt, oregano, and ¼ teaspoon of the pepper. Heat the oil in a soup pot over medium-high heat. Cook the chicken for 5 minutes on each side, or until brown. Transfer the chicken to a plate. Drain off all but 1 tablespoon of fat from the pot. Sauté the bell peppers in the same pot for 2 minutes. Squeeze the garlic from the skins and add to the pot.

**SIMMER IT LOW** Stir in the tomatoes with their juice, the broth, and chicken. Bring to a boil over high heat. Reduce the heat and simmer for 15 minutes. Stir in the onions, potatoes, corn, squash, and sage and cook for 15 minutes. Season with the salt and the remaining ¼ teaspoon pepper.

## TO ROAST GARLIC

*Preheat the oven to 400°F. Cut ½-inch off the top of the garlic and place the whole head on a 6-inch foil square. Drizzle the garlic with 1 teaspoon of olive oil, then enclose in the foil, sealing it tight. Bake for 40 minutes, or until soft. Cool.*

*Makes 4 servings*

*Per serving: 686 calories, 45g protein, 42g carbohydrates, 39g fat, 10g saturated fat, 149mg cholesterol, 930mg sodium*

# CHICKEN PEPPER POT

*Prep* **15 MINUTES**    *Cook* **31 MINUTES**

| | |
|---|---|
| 3 | medium all-purpose potatoes |
| 2 | tablespoons vegetable oil |
| 1 | cup each: diced celery, green bell pepper, and onion |
| 3 | tablespoons all-purpose flour |
| 5 | cups chicken broth |
| 2 | teaspoons hot pepper sauce |
| ½ | teaspoon each: dried thyme, ground allspice, and salt |
| ½ | pound boneless, skinless chicken breast halves |
| ¼ | cup chopped fresh parsley |

*The first pepper pot soup was prepared back in 1777 for George Washington's hungry troops, and it is still popular today. Heat up some refrigerated biscuits to make this a complete meal.*

**LET'S BEGIN** Peel and dice the potatoes. Heat the oil in a large saucepan over medium heat. Sauté the celery, green pepper, and onion for 5 minutes, or until soft. Add the potatoes and cook, stirring occasionally, 5 minutes longer.

**STIR IT IN** Stir in the flour and cook for 1 minute. Whisk in the broth, hot pepper sauce, thyme, allspice, and salt. Bring to a boil over high heat. Reduce the heat to low. Cover and simmer for 10 minutes.

**INTO THE PAN** Meanwhile, cut the chicken into bite-size pieces. Add to the vegetable mixture. Cover and simmer for 6 to 8 minutes, until the chicken is cooked through and the potatoes are tender. Stir in the chopped parsley.

*Makes 6 servings*

*Per serving: 200 calories, 15g protein, 19g carbohydrates, 6g fat, 1g saturated fat, 22mg cholesterol, 897mg sodium*

---

## Food Facts

### THE TALE OF THE BRUNSWICK STEW

Back in the days of the 1800s, politics played a big part in the social life of the colonists.

The year was 1828…the place was Brunswick County, Virginia. Dr. Creed Haskins of the Virginia state legislature asked "Uncle Jimmy" Matthews to stir up a squirrel stew (with lots and lots of onions!) to serve at a political rally. The stew was a big success. To this day, Virginia claims to have served the first Brunswick stew, although the folks living in Brunswick County in North Carolina often disagreed.

# CHICKEN, ROSEMARY, & WHITE BEAN STEW

*Prep* **20 MINUTES**     *Cook* **40 MINUTES**

4   cups cooked white kidney (cannellini) or Great Northern beans or 2 cans (19 ounces each), rinsed and drained

2   teaspoons olive oil

2   pounds chicken pieces

10  ounces pearl onions, peeled and halved

3   carrots, chopped

5   garlic cloves, minced

4   ounces Canadian bacon, diced

2   tablespoons balsamic vinegar

1   cup dry white wine

2   teaspoons chopped fresh rosemary, or ¾ teaspoon dried, crumbled

2   cups chicken broth

Salt and ground black pepper

*If you don't like peeling onions, save some time (and the tears). Substitute jarred or frozen pearl onions for the fresh. They come already trimmed and peeled and no one will ever know.*

**LET'S BEGIN** Cook the beans according to package directions. Remove the skin from all of the chicken except the wings. Heat the oil in a large nonstick soup pot over high heat. Brown the chicken on all sides. Add the onions, carrots, garlic, and bacon and sauté for 6 minutes, or until the onions are light brown.

**STIR IT IN** Stir in the vinegar and wine and bring to a boil. Reduce the heat to medium-low and simmer for 10 minutes, or until the liquid reduces by about one-third. Stir in the beans, rosemary, and broth.

**SIMMER LOW** Bring the soup back to a simmer. Cover and cook for 20 minutes to allow the flavors to blend. Season with salt and pepper.

*Makes 4 servings*
*Per serving: 681 calories, 50g protein, 52g carbohydrates, 26g fat, 8g saturated fat, 122mg cholesterol, 980mg sodium*

## Time Savers

### THE FASTEST WAY TO PEEL ONIONS

The small white pearl onions used in this stew are some of the sweetest ones around—but peeling a whole bag can take at least 15 minutes. Here's a fast tip: drop them right out of the bag into a pot of boiling water. Let them stay about a minute, or until the skins loosen. Drain the onions in a colander and rinse under cold running water. The skins slip right off.

# CURRIED CHICKEN STEW

*Prep* **10 MINUTES**     *Cook* **23 MINUTES**

*Baby-cut carrots, frozen peas, and cream of chicken soup give this quick soup rich flavor. Depending on your preference, use a mild or hot curry powder—either will be delicious.*

| | |
|---|---|
| 2 | tablespoons butter |
| 1¼ | pounds boneless, skinless chicken breast halves, cut into 1-inch pieces |
| 1 | large onion, cut lengthwise in half and sliced crosswise |
| 8 | small red potatoes, scrubbed and quartered |
| 1 | cup baby-cut carrots |
| 1½ | cups water |
| 1 | cup half-and-half |
| 1 | cup frozen peas |
| 1 | can (10¾ ounces) condensed cream of chicken soup |
| 1 | tablespoon curry powder |
| 1 | teaspoon sugar |

**LET'S BEGIN** Melt the butter in a large saucepan over medium-high heat. Sauté the chicken and onion for 3 minutes, or until the onion is soft.

**BUBBLE & STIR** Stir in the potatoes, carrots, and water. Cook, stirring occasionally, for 5 minutes, until the mixture comes to a boil.

**INTO THE PAN** Stir in all of the remaining ingredients. Reduce the heat to medium and cook 15 minutes longer, or until the vegetables are tender.

*Makes 6 servings*

*Per serving: 376 calories, 29g protein, 35g carbohydrates, 14g fat, 7g saturated fat, 84mg cholesterol, 560mg sodium*

# KICKIN' TEXAS CHILI

*Prep* **15 MINUTES**    *Cook* **1½ HOURS**

2   **pounds boneless beef sirloin or round steak**

4   **tablespoons vegetable oil**

2   **large onions, chopped**

3   **garlic cloves, minced**

1   **pound ground beef**

2   **cans (16 ounces each) whole tomatoes in purée**

1   **can (15 to 19 ounces) red kidney beans, undrained**

⅓   **cup hot pepper sauce**

¼   **cup chili powder**

2   **tablespoons ground cumin**

1   **tablespoon dried oregano**

½   **teaspoon ground black pepper**

**Shredded Cheddar cheese and chopped scallions (optional)**

*Some purists believe that chili isn't chili unless the meat's in chunks. You'll be surprised at how little time it takes to cut the beef up. This one's hot enough for Texans...or go lighter on the pepper sauce!*

**LET'S BEGIN** Cut the beef into 1-inch chunks. Heat 1 tablespoon of the oil in a large pot or Dutch oven over medium heat. Sauté the onions and garlic for 5 minutes or until soft. Transfer to a small bowl and set aside.

**BUBBLE & STIR** Heat the remaining 3 tablespoons of oil in the pot. Cook the sirloin and ground beef, in batches, over medium heat for 15 minutes, or until brown. Drain off the fat. Stir in the remaining ingredients except the Cheddar and scallions, if using. Bring to a boil over medium-high heat.

**SIMMER LOW** Return the onions and garlic to the chili and partially cover the pot. Reduce the heat and simmer for 1 hour, or until the meat is tender. Sprinkle with Cheddar cheese and scallions, if you like.

*Makes 10 servings*
*Per serving: 433 calories, 31g protein, 16g carbohydrates, 27g fat, 9g saturated fat, 91mg cholesterol, 558mg sodium*

---

## Food Facts

### KEEP A MENU OF INSTANT DINNERS IN THE FREEZER

Most soups and stews, except those with a cream base, freeze perfectly. Whenever you're making a soup or stew, simmer up a double batch. Serve half and cool the other. Ladle into resealable freezer bags (either a large one or individual ones), leaving a little extra room for expansion. To avoid spills, place the bag in a bowl then ladle in the soup. Push out the extra air and seal. Label the bags and put in the freezer on a baking sheet (this ensures the bags freeze flat and take less space). To reheat, drop the bag into a pot of simmering water until the contents are piping hot. Dinner's ready in an instant!

# OCTOBERFEST STEW

*Prep* **15 MINUTES**     *Bake* **1½ HOURS**

1    package bag 'n' season
     pot roast

2    medium all-purpose
     potatoes

2    pounds beef chuck, cut
     into 1-inch chunks

2    large onions, sliced

1    pound baby-cut carrots

1    tablespoon packed
     brown sugar

¼    teaspoon ground black
     pepper

Ground nutmeg (optional)

1    cup beer or beef broth

*In the fall in Germany, there are Octoberfests galore. Hearty stews are frequent fare. This one cooks "on its own" inside a bag.*

**LET'S BEGIN** Preheat the oven to 350°F. Place roasting bag in a 13x9-inch roasting pan. Peel and cut potatoes into 1-inch chunks and place in bag with beef, onions, and carrots.

**SEASON & SPICE** Combine the brown sugar, beef seasoning blend (from bag), pepper, and nutmeg, if using, and sprinkle it over the meat. Pour in the beer. Close the bag, tie, and poke 4 small holes in the top of bag for steam to escape.

**INTO THE OVEN** Bake for 1½ hours. Remove the pan from the oven and let rest for 5 minutes.

> *Makes 8 servings*
>
> *Per serving: 377 calories, 25g protein, 19g carbohydrates, 21g fat, 8g saturated fat, 88mg cholesterol, 470mg sodium*

# IRISH LAMB STEW

*Prep* **15 MINUTES**     *Cook* **1½ HOURS**

4    medium all-purpose
     potatoes

3    medium carrots

1    pound boneless lamb,
     cut into 1-inch pieces

1    medium onion, sliced

1    teaspoon garlic salt

½    teaspoon garlic powder

½    teaspoon ground pepper

1¼   cups water

Chopped fresh parsley
(optional)

*Irish stew is a classic, and this one is the easiest ever—no need to brown the meat. All of the ingredients are slowly simmered together to tender perfection. Add a green salad and fruit pie with cream.*

**LET'S BEGIN** Peel the potatoes and carrots and slice ½-inch thick. Combine all of the ingredients, except the parsley, in a Dutch oven. Bring to a boil over medium-high heat.

**SIMMER LOW** Reduce the heat. Cover and simmer, stirring occasionally, for 1½ hours, or until the lamb is tender. Ladle into large bowls and sprinkle with parsley, if you like.

> *Makes 4 servings*
>
> *Per serving: 367 calories, 24g protein, 30g carbohydrates, 17g fat, 8g saturated fat, 75mg cholesterol, 334mg sodium*

# BUTTERNUT, APPLE, & YOGURT SOUP

*Prep* **15 MINUTES**   *Cook* **28 MINUTES**

1   tablespoon vegetable oil

2   cups chopped onions

2   teaspoons curry powder

1   butternut squash (about 1½ pounds), halved, seeded, peeled, and diced

1   Granny Smith apple, peeled, cored, and chopped

4   cups reduced-sodium chicken broth

½   teaspoon ground cinnamon

Salt and ground black pepper

2   cups plain low-fat yogurt

3   tablespoons sunflower seeds

*Two of the best things about the fall season are fresh apples and butternut squash. Use a sweet apple instead of a Granny Smith for a slightly sweeter soup and, if you aren't counting calories, substitute sour cream or heavy cream for some of the yogurt.*

**LET'S BEGIN** Heat the oil in a large saucepan over medium heat. Sauté the onions and curry powder for 3 minutes or until the onions are soft.

**BUBBLE & STIR** Stir in the squash, apple, and broth and bring to a boil. Reduce the heat and simmer for 25 minutes.

**PROCESS IT SMOOTH** Purée the squash mixture in a blender or food processor until smooth. Return the soup to the pot. Stir in the cinnamon, season with salt and pepper, and whisk in the yogurt. Ladle into bowls and sprinkle the sunflower seeds on top.

*Makes 8 servings*
*Per serving: 141 calories, 7g protein, 20g carbohydrates, 5g fat, 1g saturated fat, 4mg cholesterol, 361mg sodium*

# FRENCH ONION AU JUS

*Prep* **10 MINUTES**     *Bake/Cook* **33 MINUTES**

| | |
|---|---|
| 2 | tablespoons butter |
| 2 | cups sliced sweet onions |
| 1 | teaspoon dried Italian seasoning |
| ½ | teaspoon cracked pepper |
| 2 | tablespoons Marsala or Madeira wine (optional) |
| 1 | package (¾ ounce) au jus gravy mix |
| 2 | cups water |
| 4 | slices French bread, toasted |
| 1 | cup shredded mozzarella cheese (4 ounces) |

*Simmer up this easy and ever-so-French onion soup. Great flavor comes from slow-cooking the onions until deep brown. Bon appetit!*

**LET'S BEGIN** Melt the butter in a large skillet over medium heat. Add the onions, Italian seasoning, and pepper. Cook, stirring often, for 25 minutes, or until the onions caramelize (turn deep brown). Add the wine, if using, the gravy mix, and water. Cook over medium-high for 5 minutes.

**SERVE IT UP** Preheat the broiler. Place individual soup crocks in the broiler pan. Ladle in the soup, top each with a toast, and sprinkle with ¼ cup mozzarella. Broil about 5 inches from the heat for 2 minutes, or until the cheese melts.

*Makes 2 servings*

*Per serving: 483 calories, 18g protein, 43g carbohydrates, 27g fat, 16g saturated fat, 80mg cholesterol, 1,880mg sodium*

*SuperQuick*
# EARLY GARDEN PEA SOUP

*Prep* **5 MINUTES**     *Cook* **18 MINUTES**

| | |
|---|---|
| ¾ | cup sliced onion |
| 1 | garlic clove, minced |
| 1 | tablespoon sweet butter |
| 2 | cans (15¼ ounces each) sweet peas (no-salt added) |
| 1 | cup milk |
| ½ | cup low-salt chicken broth |
| ½ | cup chopped parsley |
| **Dash nutmeg and pepper** | |

*Whirl up this favorite pea soup in minutes in your blender.*

**LET'S BEGIN** Sauté onion and garlic in butter in a large saucepan over medium-high heat until soft. Purée 1 can peas and milk in blender until smooth. Transfer to pan.

**WHIRL IT UP** Purée the other can of peas and all the remaining ingredients in a blender until smooth.

**SIMMER LOW** Add purée to saucepan and simmer for 15 minutes (do not boil!). Great served hot or cold.

*Per serving: 127 calories, 7g protein, 17g carbohydrates, 14g fat, 2g saturated fat, 12mg cholesterol, 496mg sodium*

*SuperQuick*
# SMOKED SALMON SOUP

*Prep* **10 MINUTES**    *Cook* **13 MINUTES**

| | |
|---|---|
| 2 | **cups baby-cut carrots** |
| 2 | **cups frozen diced potatoes with onions and peppers** |
| ½ | **cup frozen peas** |
| 3 | **tablespoons butter** |
| 3 | **tablespoons flour** |
| 3 | **cups milk** |
| 1 | **cup flaked smoked salmon** |
| ¾ | **teaspoon salt** |
| 2 | **tablespoons chopped fresh dill** |

*Here's an elegant way to serve smoked salmon—in a rich creamy soup with vegetables. It's ready to serve in less than a half hour.*

**LET'S BEGIN** Halve the carrots. Cook in water over medium-high heat in a large saucepan for 4 to 5 minutes, or until water comes to a boil. Reduce heat to medium. Add the potatoes and peas and cook 6 to 8 minutes more, until carrots are crisp-tender. Drain vegetables in a colander and set aside.

**MAKE IT SAUCY** Melt butter in the same saucepan over medium heat. Whisk in the flour and cook for 1 minute. Gradually stir in the milk and cook for 2 minutes, or until the mixture thickens. Stir in the vegetables, salmon, and salt.

**SERVE** Cook until heated through and stir in chopped dill.

*Makes 4 servings*

*Per serving: 375 calories, 16g protein, 41g carbohydrates, 17g fat, 10g saturated fat, 57mg cholesterol, 1,248mg sodium*

## On the Menu

---

**Build a meal around this soup that's easy, yet elegant enough for company**

---

Smoked Salmon Soup

Fresh Tomato Salad with White Wine Vinaigrette

Warm Croissants

Pound Cake with Berries

# SWISS & CRAB MORNAY
*Prep* **15 MINUTES**    *Cook* **8 MINUTES**

3    tablespoons butter

3    tablespoons all-purpose flour

¼    cup dry white wine or water

1    can (14½ ounces) chicken broth

1    cup heavy cream

8    ounces crabmeat (real or imitation), flaked and picked through

1    small red bell pepper, cut into thin strips

1¼    cups finely shredded Swiss cheese (5 ounces)

Chopped fresh parsley

Hot cooked spinach fettuccine (optional)

*Turn white sauce into a rich mornay soup by adding cheese and crab—in less than 20 minutes. An easy way to wow guests!*

**LET'S BEGIN**  Melt the butter in a medium saucepan over medium heat. Whisk in the flour and cook, stirring occasionally, for 1 minute, or until smooth and bubbly. Gradually stir in the wine and broth, stirring constantly for 2 minutes, or until the mixture boils and thickens.

**STIR IT IN**  Add the cream, crabmeat, and bell pepper. Reduce the heat to medium and cook for 5 minutes, or until heated through. Remove from the heat.

**SERVE IT UP**  Stir in the cheese until melted. Top with parsley and serve with fettuccine, if you like.

*Makes 5 servings*

*Per serving: 420 calories, 20g protein, 7g carbohydrates, 34g fat, 21g saturated fat, 147mg cholesterol, 560mg sodium*

# Manhattan Clam Chowder

*Prep* **15 MINUTES**  *Cook* **50 MINUTES**

| | |
|---|---|
| 2 | medium large potatoes |
| 2 | slices bacon, diced |
| 2 | large bell peppers (1 green, 1 red), diced |
| ½ | cup each: chopped carrot, celery, and onion |
| 1 | garlic clove, minced |
| 2 | cups bottled clam juice |
| 1 | cup tomato cocktail |
| 1 | large tomato, chopped |
| 1 | teaspoon oregano |
| ½ | teaspoon black pepper |
| 2 | cups fresh or canned clams, chopped (24) |

*In Rhode Island, the folks throw tomatoes into their clam chowder pot. How it got its name is a mystery, but it's served in the famous Oyster Bar in New York City. This one's an easy company supper!*

**LET'S BEGIN** Peel and dice the potatoes. Sauté the bacon, peppers, carrot, celery, onion, and garlic in a large soup pot over medium heat for 10 minutes, or until tender. (Do not brown bacon.)

**INTO THE POT** Add all of the remaining ingredients except the clams to the pot. Simmer 35 minutes longer, or until the potatoes are tender.

**STIR IT IN** Stir in the clams and cook 5 minutes longer..

*Makes 8 servings*
*Per serving: 140 calories, 14g protein, 16g carbohydrates, 2g fat, 0g saturated fat, 21mg cholesterol, 560mg sodium*

---

## Food Facts

### THE CLAM SHACK

**It's all in the shell**—It's easy to buy the right clams for the recipe go by the shell. Although clams come in a dozen varieties, they all roughly fall into two categories: hard-shell clams and soft-shells.

**Hard-shell clams**—Popular along the Atlantic coast, hard-shell clams come in three categories: Littlenecks are the smallest (about 2" the tenderest, and the sweetest. Perfect for eating raw, steaming, and using in pasta sauces. Cherrystones are medium in size (3" across) and great for baking and stuffing. Chowder clams are the largest, not as tender, but ideal for cutting up into chowders. Look for clams that are tightly closed. To clean them, scrub with a stiff brush under cold running water.

**Soft-shell clams**—These have delicate shells that don't close completely, because of their long necklike siphon protruding out. They're called "steamers" on the Eastern shore; long razor clams are found on the West Coast. When buying clams, touch the siphon gently. If it retracts slightly the clam is fresh. To remove the sand that naturally enters through the open shells, cover the clams with saltwater (1 tablespoon to 3 quarts water), refrigerate and soak at least 3 hours or overnight.

# PINEAPPLE GAZPACHO

*Prep* **25 MINUTES**     *Chill* **2 HOURS**

3   cups small fresh pineapple chunks

1   medium cucumber, peeled, seeded, and chopped

1   cup chopped yellow bell pepper

⅔   cup chopped red onion

1¼  cups pineapple juice

2   tablespoons Italian salad dressing

2   tablespoons sugar

2   tablespoons chopped fresh cilantro

1   teaspoon chopped jalapeño

*Here's the perfect icy soup to cool off a summer's evening. Make it in minutes in the morning and chill until suppertime. Great with quick grilled salmon and a slice of pound cake for dessert.*

**LET'S BEGIN**   Toss together 1 cup of the pineapple chunks, ½ cup cucumber, ½ cup bell pepper, and ⅓ cup onion in a medium bowl. Set aside.

**PROCESS IT SMOOTH**   Drop the remaining pineapple chunks, cucumber, bell pepper, and onion into a food processor or blender. Add the remaining ingredients and process until smooth.

**MIX & CHILL**   Stir into the reserved pineapple mixture. Cover and refrigerate for 2 hours, or until chilled.

*Makes 5 servings*

*Per serving: 93 calories, 1g protein, 23g carbohydrates, 0g fat, 0g saturated fat, 0mg cholesterol, 10mg sodium*

# STRAWBERRY SORBET SOUP

*Prep* **20 MINUTES**     *Chill* **2 HOURS**

2       packages (10 ounces each) frozen sliced strawberries in syrup, thawed

¾       cup sugar

¼       cup lemon juice

4       cartons (8 ounces each) strawberry low-fat yogurt

2½      cups sliced fresh strawberries

1       cup chopped peeled mango

½       cup chopped pineapple

1       cup (½ inch) cubes low-fat pound cake, broiled until toasted

Mint sprigs (optional)

*What's for dessert? Strawberry soup topped with fresh berry sorbet.*

**LET'S BEGIN** To make sorbet, drain frozen strawberries, reserving 1 cup juice. Process the drained berries, ¼ cup of the sugar, lemon juice, and 1 carton yogurt in a food processor or blender, or until smooth. Pour mixture into an 8-inch square baking dish. Cover and freeze until firm, stirring occasionally.

**INTO THE PAN** Heat the reserved strawberry juice and the remaining sugar in a small saucepan over medium-high heat until sugar is dissolved. Cool. Process 1½ cups of fresh berries, mango, pineapple, and remaining yogurt until smooth.

**CHILL & SERVE** Transfer to a bowl, cover, and chill for 2 hours. Sspoon into bowls and top with sorbet, cake cubes, and remaining fresh strawberries. Garnish with mint, if desired.

*Makes 8 servings*
*Per serving: 357 calories, 7g protein, 77g carbohydrates, 4g fat, 2g saturated fat, 21mg cholesterol, 157mg sodium*

# CREDITS

PAGE 2 Hormel: Photo for Italian Pepperoni Minestrone courtesy of Hormel Foods. Used with permission.

PAGE 8 Land O'Lakes: Photo for Brunswick Stew courtesy of Land O'Lakes, Inc. Used with permission.

PAGE 12/101 Birds Eye: Recipe and photo for Texas Beef Stew courtesy of Birds Eye Foods. Used with permission.

PAGE 16 Campbell Soup Company: Photo for Garlicky Potato-Leek Soup courtesy of Campbell Soup Company. Used with permission.

PAGE 18 Del Monte: Recipe for Chicken-Tarragon Soup courtesy of Del Monte Foods. Used with permission.

PAGE 19 USA Rice Federation: Recipe and photo for Hearty Chicken & Rice Bowl courtesy of the USA Rice Federation. Used with permission.

PAGE 20 McCormick: Recipe for Fiery Rice 'n' Bean Pot courtesy of McCormick. Used with permission.

PAGES 20/21 McIlhenny Company: Recipe and photo for 30-Minute Chili Pot courtesy of McIlhenny Company. Used with permission.

PAGE 22 McCormick: Recipe and photo for Touchdown Chili courtesy of McCormick. Used with permission.

PAGE 23 Tropicana: Recipe and photo for Golden-Glow Soup courtesy of Tropicana Products, Inc. Used with permission.

PAGE 24/25 French's: Recipe and photo for Creamy Corn Bisque courtesy of Frank's® RedHot® Cayenne Pepper Sauce. Used with permission.

PAGE 26 Almond Board of California: Recipe for Broccoli-Cheddar Soup Amandine courtesy of the Almond Board of California. Used with permission.

PAGE 27 Campbell Soup Company: Recipe for Garlicky Potato-Leek Soup courtesy of Campbell Soup Company. Used with permission.

PAGE 28 National Sunflower Association: Recipe and photo for Onion Soup with Roasted Sunflower Kernels courtesy of the National Sunflower Association. Used with permission.

PAGE 29 Dannon: Recipe for Sherried Pumpkin Soup courtesy of The Dannon Company, Inc. Used with permission.

PAGE 30/31 Dannon: Recipe and photo for Sweet Potato & Yogurt Soup courtesy of The Dannon Company, Inc. Used with permission.

PAGE 32 National Pork Board: Recipe for Bow-Tie Sausage Pot courtesy of the National Pork Board. Used with permission.

PAGE 32/33 National Pork Board: Recipe and photo for BLT Bowl courtesy of the National Pork Board. Used with permission.

PAGE 34 Jenny Craig: Recipe and photo for Summer Tomato Bowl courtesy of Jenny Craig, Inc. Used with permission.

PAGE 36/37 McIlhenny Company: Recipe and photo for Turkey-Vegetable Soup courtesy of McIlhenny Company. Used with permission.

PAGE 38 Dannon: Recipe for Creamy Vegetable Cup courtesy of The Dannon Company, Inc. Used with permission.

PAGE 38 Jenny Craig: Recipe for Mac & Vegetable Pot courtesy of Jenny Craig, Inc. Used with permission.

PAGE 39 Almond Board of California: Recipe for Garden Vegetable Soup courtesy of the Almond Board of California. Used with permission.

PAGE 40 8th Continent: Recipe and photo for Broccoli-Cheese Bowl courtesy of 8th Continent, LLC. 8TH CONTINENT® trademark used with permission.

PAGE 41 Dannon: Recipe for Carrot Soup courtesy of The Dannon Company, Inc. Used with permission.

PAGE 42 French's: Recipe for Hearty Tortellini Pot courtesy of French's® Worcestershire Sauce. Used with permission.

PAGE 43 Almond Board of California: Recipe for Zucchini-Pesto Soup courtesy of the Almond Board of California. Used with permission.

PAGE 44 Kraft Foods: Recipe for Creamy Squash Soup courtesy of Kraft Kitchens. Used with permission.

PAGE 44/45 Dole: Recipe for Asparagus Lemon Soup courtesy of Dole Food Company. Used with permission.

PAGE 46 McCormick: Recipe for Tropical Seafood Stew courtesy of McCormick. Used with permission.

PAGE 47 Tone Brothers: Recipe for Shrimp Gazpacho courtesy of Tone Brothers, Inc., producer of Tone's, Spice Islands, and Durkee products. (Photo appears on back cover.) Used with permission.

PAGE 47 McIlhenny Company: Recipe for Avocado-Orange Cup courtesy of McIlhenny Company. Used with permission.

PAGE 48 McIlhenny Company: Recipe and photo for Zesty Green Gazpacho courtesy of McIlhenny Company. Used with permission.

PAGE 49 French's: Recipe for Garden-Fresh Red Gazpacho courtesy of Frank's® RedHot® Cayenne Pepper Sauce. Used with permission.

PAGE 50/51 Jenny Craig: Recipe and photo for Summer Tomato Bowl courtesy of Jenny Craig, Inc. Used with permission.

PAGE 51 Land O'Lakes: Photo for Creamy Tomato Soup courtesy of Land O'Lakes, Inc. Used with permission.

PAGE 52 Land O'Lakes: Photo for Roasted Corn Chowder courtesy of Land O'Lakes, Inc. Used with permission.

PAGE 54 Perdue: Recipe and photo for Chicken & Red Pepper Corn Chowder courtesy of ©Perdue Farms. Used with permission.

PAGE 55 Land O'Lakes: Recipe for Roasted-Corn Chowder courtesy of Land O'Lakes, Inc. Used with permission.

PAGE 56/57 McIlhenny Company: Recipe and photo for Coconut Chicken Chowder courtesy of McIlhenny Company. Used with permission.

PAGE 58/59 Hormel: Recipe and photo for Ham and Vegetable Stew courtesy of Hormel Foods. Used with permission.

PAGE 60 Del Monte: Recipe for Black Bean Chili Chowder courtesy of Del Monte Foods. Used with permission.

PAGE 60 Kraft Foods: Recipe for Midwest Cheese Pot courtesy of Kraft Kitchens. Used with permission.

PAGE 61 Kraft Foods: Recipe for Down East Fish Chowder courtesy of Kraft Kitchens. Used with permission.

PAGE 62/63 StarKist: Recipe and photo for Tuna Corn Chowdah courtesy of StarKist®. StarKist is a registered trademark of Del Monte Foods, © 2003. All rights reserved. Used with permission.

PAGE 64 Kraft Foods: Recipe for Slim 'n' Sassy Corn Chowder courtesy of Kraft Kitchens. Used with permission.

PAGE 64 Kraft Foods: Recipe for American Chowder courtesy of Kraft Kitchens. Used with permission.

PAGE 65 McCormick: Recipe and photo for Potato-Corn Chowder with Chicken courtesy of McCormick. Used with permission.

PAGE 66 Hormel: Recipe and Photo for Peppy Baked Potato Soup courtesy of Hormel Foods. Used with permission.

PAGE 67 McIlhenny Company: Recipe for Leek & Potato Pot courtesy of McIlhenny Company. Used with permission.

PAGE 68 Hormel: Photo for Italian Pepperoni Minestrone courtesy of Hormel Foods. Used with permission.

PAGE 70 Perdue: Recipe and photo for Sante Fe Chicken Soup courtesy of ©Perdue Farms. Used with permission.

PAGE 72 McCormick: Recipe for Greek Avgolemono Soup with Chicken courtesy of McCormick. Used with permission.

PAGE 73 McCormick: Recipe for Tortilla Chicken Chili courtesy of McCormick. Used with permission.

PAGE 74 Kraft Foods: Recipe for Mexican Taco Stew courtesy of Kraft Kitchens. Used with permission.

PAGE 75 McCormick: Recipe for Coconut Shrimp Stew courtesy of McCormick. Used with permission.

PAGE 76/77 French's: Recipe and photo for Spicy Senegalese Soup courtesy of Frank's® RedHot® Cayenne Pepper Sauce. Used with permission.

PAGE 78 Kraft Foods: Recipe for Zuppe di Pesce courtesy of Kraft Kitchens. Used with permission.

PAGE 79 Kraft Foods: Recipe for Chicken Rice Gumbo courtesy of Kraft Kitchens. Used with permission.

PAGE 79 Campbell Soup Company: Recipe for Spanish Seafood Stew courtesy of Campbell Soup Company. Used with permission.

PAGE 80/81 USA Rice Federation: Recipe and photo for Tuscany Rice and Bean Soup courtesy of the USA Rice Federation. Used with permission.

PAGE 82 Hormel: Recipe for Italian Pepperoni Minestrone courtesy of Hormel Foods. Used with permission.

PAGE 83 Almond Board of California: Recipe for Cold Spanish Vegetable Soup courtesy of the Almond Board of California. Used with permission.

PAGE 84 Almond Board of California: Recipe and photo for Spanish Almond-Onion Soup courtesy of the Almond Board of California. Used with permission.

PAGE 86 McIlhenny Company: Recipe and photo for Greek Pilaf courtesy of McIlhenny Company. Used with permission.

PAGE 87 National Chicken Council: Recipe and photo for Warming Asian Chicken Soup courtesy of the National Chicken Council/U.S. Poultry & Egg Association. Used with permission.

PAGE 88 French's: Photo for Hoppin John courtesy of Frank's® RedHot® Cayenne Pepper Sauce. Used with permission.

PAGE 90/91 Hormel: Recipe and photo for Hearty Black Bean Bowl courtesy of Hormel Foods. Used with permission.

PAGE 92 Kikkoman: Recipe for Tuscan Chicken & White Bean Pot courtesy of Kikkoman. Used with permission.

PAGE 93 Kraft Foods: Recipe for Mac 'n' Double Cheese Soup courtesy of Kraft Kitchens. Used with permission.

PAGE 94/95 Kikkoman: Recipe and photo for Big Bowl of Red courtesy of Kikkoman. Used with permission.

PAGE 95 Lawry's: Recipe for Soul City Chili courtesy of Lawry's Foods. Used with permission.

PAGE 96 McCormick: Recipe and photo for American Chili Pot courtesy of McCormick. Used with permission.

PAGE 97 Birds Eye: Recipe for Tina's Taco Soup courtesy of Birds Eye Foods. Used with permission.

PAGE 98 McCormick: Recipe for Ham 'n' Cheese Kettle courtesy of McCormick. Used with permission.

PAGE 98/99 National Pork Board: Recipe and photo for Italian Cupboard Stew courtesy of the National Pork Board. Used with permission.

PAGE 100 Campbell Soup Company: Recipe for Slow-Cooker Tuscan Beef Stew courtesy of Campbell Soup Company. Used with permission.

PAGE 101 Kraft Foods: Recipe for Midwestern Cheese Pot courtesy of Kraft Kitchens. Used with permission.

PAGE 102 French's: Recipe and photo for Beefy Meal-in-a-Pot courtesy of French's® Worcestershire Sauce. Used with permission.

PAGE 103 McCormick: Recipe and photo for Quick and Easy Beef Stew courtesy of McCormick. Used with permission.

PAGE 104/105 National Pork Board: Recipe and photo for Smoky Pasta & Bean Soup courtesy of the National Pork Board. Used with permission.

PAGE 106 Lawry's: Recipe for White Bean, Chicken and Chili Pot courtesy of Lawry's Foods. Used with permission.

PAGE 107 Birds Eye: Recipe and photo for Shrimp Creole courtesy of Birds Eye Foods. Used with permission.

PAGE 107 Bertolli: Weekday Seafood Chowder courtesy of Unilever Bestfoods North America. Used with permission.

PAGE 108 French's: Recipe for Hoppin' John Soup courtesy of Frank's® RedHot® Cayenne Pepper Sauce. Used with permission.

PAGE 109 Hormel: Recipe for Ham and Barley Cream Soup courtesy of Hormel Foods. Used with permission.

PAGE 110/111 National Pork Board: Recipe and photo for Pork and Pepper Stew courtesy of the National Pork Board. Used with permission.

PAGE 112/113 Hormel: Recipe and photo for Zesty Italian Soup courtesy of Hormel Foods. Used with permission.

PAGE 114 Birds Eye: Recipe for Italian Sausage Stew courtesy of Birds Eye Foods. Used with permission.

PAGE 115 United States Potato Board: Recipe for Moroccan-Style Chicken & Potato Tagine courtesy of the United States Potato Board. Used with permission.

PAGE 116 National Pork Board: Recipe for Country Cupboard Kettle courtesy of the National Pork Board. Used with permission.

PAGE 116/117 Perdue: Recipe and photo for Toasty Tomato and Chicken Stew courtesy of ©Perdue Farms. Used with permission.

PAGE 118 Land O'Lakes: Photo for Brunswick Stew courtesy of Land O'Lakes, Inc. Used with permission.

PAGE 120/121 National Chicken Council: Recipe and photo for Best-Ever Chicken Noodle courtesy of the National Chicken Council/U.S. Poultry & Egg Association. Used with permission.

PAGE 122 Pillsbury: Recipe for Biscuit-topped Hamburger Stew courtesy of The Pillsbury Company, a subsidiary of General Mills, Inc. Used with permission.

PAGE 123 Bush's Best Beans: Recipe and photo for Caribbean One-Pot courtesy of Bush's Best® Beans. Used with permission.

PAGE 124 Land O'Lakes: Recipe for Brunswick Stew courtesy of Land O'Lakes, Inc. Used with permission.

PAGE 125 McIlhenny Company: Recipe for Chicken Pepper Pot courtesy of McIlhenny Company. Used with permission.

PAGE 126/127 National Chicken Council: Recipe and photo for Chicken Rosemary & White Bean Stew courtesy of the National Chicken Council/U.S. Poultry & Egg Association. Used with permission.

PAGE 128/129 Land O'Lakes: Recipe and photo for Curried Chicken Stew courtesy of Land O'Lakes, Inc. Used with permission.

PAGE 130 French's: Recipe for Kickin' Texas Chili courtesy of Frank's® RedHot® Cayenne Pepper Sauce. Used with permission.

PAGE 131 McCormick: Recipe for Octoberfest Stew courtesy of McCormick. Used with permission.

PAGE 131 Tone Brothers: Recipe for Irish Lamb Stew courtesy of Tone Brothers, Inc., producer of Tone's, Spice Islands, and Durkee products. Used with permission.

PAGE 132 Dannon: Recipe and photo for Butternut, Apple, and Yogurt Soup courtesy of The Dannon Company, Inc. Used with permission.

PAGE 133 Tone Brothers: Recipe for French Onion au Jus courtesy of Tone Brothers, Inc., producer of Tone's, Spice Islands, and Durkee products. Used with permission.

PAGE 133 Del Monte: Recipe for Early Garden Pea soup courtesy of Del Monte Foods. Used with permission.

PAGE 134 Land O'Lakes: Recipe and photo for Smoked Salmon Soup courtesy of Land O'Lakes, Inc. Used with permission.

PAGE 135 Land O'Lakes: Recipe and photo for Swiss & Crab Mornay courtesy of Land O'Lakes, Inc. Used with permission.

PAGE 136/137 Clamato: Recipe and photo for Manhattan Clam Chowder courtesy of Clamato Tomato Cocktail. Used with permission.

PAGE 138 Dole: Recipe and photo for Pineapple Gazpacho courtesy of Dole Food Company. Used with permission.

PAGE 139 California Strawberry Commission: Recipe and photo for Strawberry Sorbet Soup courtesy of the ©California Strawberry Commission. All rights reserved. Used with permission.

BACK COVER Tone Brothers: Photo for Shrimp Gazpacho courtesy of Tone Brothers, Inc., producer of Tone's, Spice Islands, and Durkee products. Used with permission.

# WEBSITES

RODALE INC.
www.rodale.com

Almond Board of California
www.AlmondsAreIn.com

Bertolli
www.Bertolli.com

Birds Eye
www.birdseyefoods.com

Bush's Best Beans
www.bushbeans.com

California Strawberry Commission
www.calstrawberry.com

Campbell Soup Company
www.campbellskitchen.com

Clamato
www.clamato.com

Dannon
www.dannon.com

Del Monte
www.delmonte.com

Dole
www.dole.com

8th Continent
www.8thcontinent.com

French's & Red Hot
www.frenchsfoods.com

Hormel
www.hormel.com

Jenny Craig
www.jennycraig.com

Kikkoman
www.kikkoman-usa.com

Kraft Foods
www.kraftfoods.com

Land O'Lakes
www.landolakes.com

Lawry's
www.lawrys.com

McCormick
www.mccormick.com

McIlhenny Company
www.tabasco.com

National Chicken Council
www.eatchicken.com

National Pork Board
www.otherwhitemeat.com

National Sunflower Association
www.sunflowernsa.com

Perdue
www.perdue.com

Pillsbury
www.pillsbury.com

Starkist
www.starkist.com

Tone Brothers
www.spiceadvice.com

Tropicana
www.tropicana.com

USA Rice Federation
www.ricecafe.com

United States Potato Board
www.potatohelp.com

# INDEX